KU-482-233

BRILLIANT
BAKES

Si King & Dave Myers

THE HAIRY BIKERS

BRILLIANT
BAKES

'If I knew you were coming, I'd have baked a cake.'

That's what the old song says and it's dead right. Whether a chocolate cake, a simple loaf or a savoury pie, baking is an expression of love. It delivers on all counts – the anticipation, the aroma, the eating.

Some years ago, we were lucky enough to meet the late, great actor and comedian Ronnie Corbett. His father had been a master baker and Ronnie himself made good bread. He told us that when he visited friends, he would always take along a loaf of home-made bread, rather than wine or chocolates. 'It always goes down much better than anything else,' he said. And we agree. You put yourself into a home bake, it's something to share, something really special.

Nothing says home, welcome and comfort like baking – that might sound like a cliché, but it's true. Ask any estate agent and they'll tell you that the smell of a loaf of bread cooking in the oven can help them sell a house. We've always had a great tradition of baking in this country and in recent years that has only grown stronger – particularly during the pandemic when many people were at home more and maybe had a bit of extra time on their hands. We're all embracing and enjoying baking more than ever.

When we first started on our Hairy Biker career, we did three TV series that involved us being on the road in different countries and cooking with charcoal ovens and a gas jet. Not much room for baking! But we both love making bread and cakes and we love our pies, so in 2008 we pitched an idea for a series featuring us travelling around the UK, discovering the best bread, cakes, pies and so on. That series was called the *Hairy Bakers* and we learned a lot – and had fun. A few years later we filmed a series called *Bakeation* in which we visited various European countries and investigated their baking traditions. But what we've been hankering for recently is the chance to get back to the baking culture we know and love from our childhoods, the baking that's part of our heritage, and that's what this book is all about – some much-loved classics, some twists on old favourites and plenty of brand-new ideas we know you're going to enjoy.

One of the things that we love about baking is the strongly regional nature of it. To name just a few, there are the stotties of Newcastle, Grasmere gingerbread from Cumbria, the gipsy tart of Kent, bannocks in Scotland, saffron buns in Cornwall, Welsh cakes and Lincolnshire plum bread. Recently we heard about pinkies. Pinkies are a sort of

sponge cake with jam and pink icing and there's a whole culture around them, but only in Sunderland. There are fiercely fought competitions to find out who makes the best pinkies. Who knew?

And let's not forget: baking is not all about cakes and biscuits. There are so many wonderful savoury bakes – think of cheese, onion and potato pies, meat pasties, cheesy biscuits. When we were growing up, every northern household had a special plate for making plate pies – usually an old one, probably a bit chipped. The pie had a filling of mince and was served with chips. We both still love our plate pies.

Another important point is that somehow, home-made is always best. Sausage rolls are a great example. Even if you just squeeze the meat from a good sausage and wrap it up in some bought puff pastry, they will still be incredible. Everyone loves them and no shop-bought roll can compare. And that home-baked loaf of bread that you slice before you really should, still warm from the oven, gives you more of a thrill than anything you can buy.

So, big love to all of you out there with flour in your hair and pastry on your fingers. We hope you enjoy making these bakes as much as we've enjoyed creating them.

Si

Some of my very earliest memories are to do with baking – the smell of baking in the house, helping my mam make the bread. We never bought bread or cakes or biscuits, everything was made at home. And if Mam didn't have time, my Auntie Hilda would rock up with something. There was always cake. Eventually, Ginny, my older sister, got into it all too – it was part of the culture of our household. Auntie Hilda was the best baker in our family. Anything she baked, whether bread, shortbread, pies, cakes – anything you put in the oven – was always great.

I remember giving Mam a hand in the kitchen from the age of about four or five, and after my dad died when I was only eight, cooking together was a way of bonding, of spending time together. Baking is a great way of getting little kids involved with food – weighing out ingredients, stirring, mixing and – best of all – licking the bowl! There was always that treat at the end of the process. Mam always used to say that some people had bread hands, while others had pastry hands. I've got bread hands while Dave has a lighter touch and is better with the more delicate stuff. He can cope with patisserie!

In our house when I was growing up, Monday was washing day and bread day. I've never managed to make bread as good as my mam's. She had a big creamware bowl for the dough and she'd always use fresh yeast. We had a coal fire in the living room, and she'd put the dough in front of it to prove. She'd make baps which were so floury and light and as soon as they were cool enough, we'd split them and eat them with lots of butter. They were some of the finest things I've ever eaten, and I've never managed to make anything quite as good. Maybe I need that whiff of detergent that was always in our kitchen on baking day!

Mam had a book of Be-Ro home recipes that came with Be-Ro flour. She'd make a loaf to last through the week and she'd do an amazing Victoria sponge with a raspberry jam and buttercream filling. She couldn't use fresh cream as we didn't have a fridge.

My Auntie Marion liked to bake too. I remember one day when I was about seven or eight, she came round with my cousin Tony who was older than me, probably in his teens. Auntie Marion had brought this blackcurrant tart that she'd made, and I was looking forward to it. But Tony had a warning: 'David,' he said, 'My mother's pastry is like cricket pads.' And he was right! Auntie Marion could never make pastry, but she tried and that's what counts. Maybe she just didn't have pastry hands.

BAKING – THE KNOWLEDGE

We'd like to share some of the baking knowledge that we've picked up over our years of cooking on and off screen – little tips that might save you some time or heartache.

Baking is a bit different from other cooking – there's sort of alchemy to it, some magic that happens in the oven – but you do have to be accurate and measure your ingredients properly. There's less of the winging it that you can get away with when making a soup or a casserole. That said, even if your cake sinks a little or your beautiful loaf has a crack in the middle, it will still taste wonderful and you'll feel a real sense of achievement. So here goes!

EQUIPMENT

We don't want anyone to feel they have to race out and spend loads of money but there are some basic bits of kit you'll need.

Scales: Accurate measurements are important when baking and a good set of scales is essential. You'll need some measuring spoons too and a measuring jug.

Tins: A couple of baking trays are essential and, depending on what you decide to bake, you might also need a large (900g) loaf tin, a 20–21cm square baking tin for brownies and the like, a 12-hole muffin tin and a 12-hole cupcake tin. If you want to make mini fairy cakes, you'll need a 24-hole tin. It's also good to have a couple of 20cm sandwich tins for Victoria sponge-type cakes and a larger 23cm cake tin. For sweet and savoury tarts, a 23cm and a 25cm tin will be useful.

Gadgets: You can, of course, do everything by hand like our mams used to do, but you might like a bit of help. A food processor is great for making pastry and an electric hand whisk makes short work of creaming butter and sugar and whisking egg whites. If you're lucky enough to have a stand mixer, you can use if for more or less everything, including kneading dough. The stand mixer paddle is brilliant for pastry – less water is needed so the pastry is nice and short and there is less shrinkage.

SMALL ITEMS

A rubber or silicone spatula: This really helps when scraping cake batter out of the mixing bowl. Spatulas are not expensive and they work much better than a spoon.

Metal dough scrapers: Great for cleaning work surfaces and cutting dough into portions. They're also useful for cutting up tray bakes, such as brownies, into neat squares.

Pastry guide sticks or strips: These help you roll your pastry out to an even thickness which gives the best results. They're inexpensive and usually available in sets of several different sizes.

A pastry brush: Handy for brushing pies and other bakes with beaten egg or adding glaze to cakes.

Liners: It's really important to line cake tins and baking tins, so your delicious creations don't stick. Make sure you have some baking parchment, which is available in rolls or cut to rounds of different sizes. Even better is to invest in some reusable, washable liners that you can cut to fit your baking tins and use again and again.

A set of cookie cutters: You'll need these for cutting out scones and biscuits. And we find that a pizza wheel is the best thing for cutting pastry neatly.

INGREDIENTS

Flour: Flour does go off eventually, so keep an eye on use-by dates. Plain bleached white flour keeps better than most, but strong white flour does deteriorate and loses its potency, so will affect the quality of your bake. Wholemeal flour tends to go rancid if stored for too long.

Flour doesn't always need sieving, but a litte tip is to put it in your bowl with any other similar ingredients, such as baking powder, and give it a quick whisk with a balloon whisk. This gets rid of any lumps, brings in some air and makes sure everything is well combined. Less mess than sieving too.

Nuts: Shelled nuts also go rancid quite quickly, so if you buy a big bag, wrap them well and store them in the freezer to keep them fresh.

Salt: Adding a good pinch of salt to sweet as well as savoury bakes really does make a difference to the flavour balance. It also helps to lighten things like meringues.

Butter: We like to use unsalted butter in our bakes. The amount of salt in the salted products varies a lot, so we prefer to add salt separately.

Sugar: Caster sugar is the sugar most commonly used in cakes and we often use golden caster sugar which is slightly less refined and adds nice colour. Soft dark and light brown sugar are also popular and bring a touch of caramel flavour. Brown sugar does have a tendency to go rock hard in your cupboard, though. If this happens to you, put the sugar in a bowl, cover it with a damp tea towel and leave it overnight. The sugar will absorb the moisture from the tea towel and will be lovely and soft again. And if you're about to make a cake and find you've run out of icing sugar, just blitz some caster sugar in a food processor until it is fine and powdery.

Eggs: We always used to buy large eggs, but now we've discovered that the boxes of mixed eggs you see in the supermarket nowadays are quite a bit cheaper, so we go for those. We've tested all these recipes and found that the size of eggs makes no difference, so no worries. Always check that your eggs are at room temperature before using – they will beat much more successfully.

A FEW TIPS

Pastry: Pastry needs to be kept cool, so make sure your butter is cold, any water is ice cold and, if mixing by hand, your hands are cool. The advantage of using a food processor or stand mixer, of course, is that you are touching the pastry less, so it's less likely to get warm.

It's important to chill pastry properly otherwise it will shrink when baked, but don't chill it for too long or it will be too hard to roll. When making things like pastry cases, it's best to roll out the pastry, line the tin or tins, then chill. Otherwise wrap the pastry or put it in a container before chilling. If it does get a bit dry, wet your hands with really cold water and gently massage the pastry to soften it again before rolling it out.

Bread: When putting your ingredients into your mixing bowl, add the flour first, then the yeast and stir. Then add the salt – if the salt comes into too much contact with the yeast it inhibits its action.

Creaming butter and sugar: Creaming is simply beating butter and sugar together. Always use very soft butter and don't beat for more than two minutes. If you beat for too long, too much air will be incorporated into the mixture and your cake won't rise as well.

Beating egg whites: When you want dry, stiff peaks for things like meringues, beat the egg whites until they cling to the bowl and won't even move a millimetre. Hold the bowl over your head if you dare!

Measuring sticky items: When you're measuring out tablespoons of ingredients like treacle, honey or golden syrup, either dip the spoon in freshly boiled water first or rub it lightly with oil. Then whatever you are measuring will slide off the spoon easily.

Cutting/slicing: When you're cutting your bake, remove it from the tin first so you can get to the edges properly. Ideally, use a knife that is the length of the cut you need to make, so you can press it down rather than drag it through. You will get a cleaner cut that way. It also helps to lightly oil the knife blade first or dip it in some freshly boiled water. Don't use a hot knife with chocolate or anything else that might melt.

SAVO
B

OURY AKES

ASPARAGUS & RICOTTA TART

We love a savoury tart, and asparagus and ricotta are a perfect match. With some shop-bought puff pastry – preferably the all-butter kind – this is dead easy to put together and tastes amazing. Just the thing for a summer lunch.

Serves 4

1 x 320g pack of ready-rolled
   puff pastry
1 egg, beaten
150g ricotta
zest of 1 lemon
25g Parmesan, grated,
   plus extra to finish
2 bunches of asparagus
1 tbsp olive oil
squeeze of lemon juice,
   plus extra to finish
a few basil, mint or chervil
   leaves or any micro herbs,
   to garnish
salt and black pepper

Preheat the oven to 200°C/Fan 180°C/Gas 6. Unroll the puff pastry on to a lined baking tray. Score a 1.5–2cm border all the way around the pastry, making sure not to cut all the way through. Brush the whole thing with some of the beaten egg, then prick all over the centre with a fork.

Bake the pastry in the preheated oven for 15 minutes, then remove it and set it aside to cool.

Put the rest of the beaten egg in a bowl and add the ricotta. Mix until smooth, then beat in the lemon zest and Parmesan. Season well with salt and pepper.

Gently press down the centre of the pastry if it has puffed up a lot, then carefully spread with the ricotta mixture. Trim the asparagus spears so they will fit the tart. Put the olive oil in a bowl and add the asparagus, then squeeze over some lemon juice. Gently turn the spears over until they are well coated in the oil and lemon, then season with salt and pepper. Arrange the asparagus over the ricotta and grate a little more Parmesan on top.

Bake in the oven (200°C/Fan 180°C/Gas 6) for 15 minutes until the pastry is golden, the ricotta has puffed up very slightly around the asparagus and the asparagus is just cooked through. Squeeze more lemon juice over the top, sprinkle with the herbs and serve warm.

CHEESE, ONION & POTATO PIE

A really satisfying pie, this makes a cracking supper served hot with some green veg or northern-style with a plate of chips. It's also really nice served at room temperature for lunch, perhaps with a tomato salad on the side. Makes a great picnic dish too, as it's robust and doesn't break up easily.

Serves 6

Pastry
300g self-raising flour, plus
    extra for dusting
pinch of salt
75g butter, chilled and diced
75g lard, chilled and diced
    (or another 75g butter)
1 egg, beaten
2 tsp Marmite (optional)
2 tbsp cold milk

Filling
400g potatoes, boiled and
    cooled
200g hard cheese (Cheddar,
    Caerphilly or Gruyère), grated
1 onion, finely chopped
small bunch of parsley or dill,
    finely chopped
salt and black pepper

First make the pastry. Put the flour in a bowl with a good pinch of salt and add the butter and the lard, if using. Rub the fat in until the mixture resembles fine breadcrumbs, then add all but a tablespoon of the egg. If using the Marmite, whisk it into the milk, then drizzle this into the pastry, mixing until you have a firm dough. Alternatively, just add enough milk to bind the pastry together, making sure it isn't crumbly.

Dust your work surface with flour. Take two-thirds of the dough and roll it out to fill a 20cm round cake or pie tin. Put the pastry-lined tin and the remaining dough in the fridge to chill until ready to fill.

For the filling, slice the cooked potatoes quite thinly. Mix the grated cheese, onion and herbs together in a bowl and season with plenty of black pepper and a generous pinch of salt. Preheat the oven to 200°C/Fan 180°C/Gas 6.

To assemble the pie, press about a third of the cheese mixture over the base layer of pastry. Top with a layer of potatoes, then repeat with another layer of the cheese mixture. Add a second layer of the potatoes, then top with the rest of the cheese mixture. Press everything down quite firmly.

Roll out the remaining pastry and use it to top your pie. Trim and crimp the edges together and cut a couple of steam holes in the top. Brush the pie with the reserved tablespoon of egg.

Bake the pie in the oven for about 30 minutes until the filling is piping hot and the pastry is golden.

SUMMER VEGETABLE STRUDEL

Strudels don't have to be apple. This is like an English summer vegetable garden in a crispy filo coat. We first cooked it on our series *Go North* in a polytunnel at a market garden in Cumbria to show off their beautiful produce. And by golly, it certainly does.

Serves 6

Filling

2 tbsp olive oil
15g butter
200g leeks, sliced
1 tarragon sprig
200g small courgettes, sliced or diced depending on size
50ml vermouth or white wine
2 small little gem lettuces or equivalent, cut into wedges
200g runner beans, shredded
125g new potatoes, boiled whole and diced
100g tomatoes, roughly chopped
mix of fresh herbs – tarragon leaves, chervil, basil and dill, roughly chopped, or summer savoury, lemon thyme, chives and oregano, finely chopped
salt and black pepper

Crust

1 x 270g pack of filo pastry
75g butter, melted

Put a tablespoon of the oil and the butter in a large sauté pan. When the butter is foaming, add the leeks and tarragon sprig. Cook over a medium-high heat for 5 minutes, stirring regularly, until the leeks are lightly browned and starting to tenderise.

Add the courgettes and cook for another couple of minutes. Season with plenty of salt and pepper and turn up the heat. Pour in the vermouth or wine and bring to the boil. Then turn down the heat and simmer until the leeks are nice and tender – the courgettes should still have some bite to them. Leave to cool.

Toss the lettuce in the remaining olive oil and season with salt and pepper. Heat a griddle pan and griddle the lettuce over a medium heat until lightly browned but still al dente in the core. Roughly chop the wedges and add them to the leek mixture.

Bring a saucepan of water to the boil, add a pinch of salt and the runner beans. Bring the water back to the boil, then cook for a couple of minutes, then drain and run the beans under cold water to stop the cooking.

Gently stir the runner beans, potatoes, tomatoes and herbs into the leek mixture. Taste for seasoning and leave to cool completely.

Preheat the oven to 200°C/Fan 180°C/Gas 6. To assemble, take a sheet of filo and lay it landscape fashion (with the long side nearest to you) on your work surface. Brush it with butter. Lay another sheet on top and brush with more butter. Continue until you have used all the sheets, brushing generously with butter each time and sprinkling with salt every so often.

Pile the filling into the middle of the pastry, leaving a border on either side. Fold up the bottom section of pastry over the filling, then fold in the sides and very carefully roll over. If this is too unwieldy, pull the top exposed pastry over filling. Brush all over with butter, then transfer to a baking tray.

Bake in the preheated oven for 25–30 minutes until the pastry is crisp and golden brown. Best served at room temperature.

MAC & CHEESE PIE

Carbs and more carbs – this is a deeply comforting dish. The Scottish macaroni cheese pie is a chip shop staple and for centuries the Italians have enjoyed a cheese and pasta pie – ours falls somewhere in between the two. Just be sure to bake the pastry first, as the filling needs to be used as soon as it is made and you don't want to put hot filling into raw pastry. No one likes a soggy bottom!

Serves 4

Pastry

250g plain flour, plus extra
    for dusting
½ tsp baking powder
pinch of salt
1 tsp mustard powder
65g butter, chilled and diced
60g suet
about 4 tbsp iced water

Filling

225g macaroni
25g butter
1 onion, finely chopped
100g smoked bacon, finely
    chopped
2 garlic cloves, finely chopped
2 bay leaves
1 thyme sprig
20g flour
1 tsp mustard powder
1 tsp mild curry powder
    (optional)
500ml milk
75g Cheddar, grated
25g block mozzarella, grated
½ tsp chilli flakes
100g cherry tomatoes, halved
    (optional)

Topping

50g Cheddar, grated
25g block mozzarella, grated

First make the pastry. Put the flour and baking powder into a bowl and add a generous pinch of salt and the mustard powder. Rub the butter and suet into the flour until the mixture resembles fine breadcrumbs, then add just enough of the iced water to bind it together. Knead the dough very lightly to make sure it is smooth.

Dust your work surface with flour and roll out the pastry to line a 1-litre pie dish. Trim the edges around the rim, then put the pastry in the fridge to chill for at least an hour.

Preheat the oven to 180°C/Fan 160°C/Gas 4. Prick the base of the pie with a fork, then line it with baking parchment and fill it with baking beans. Bake the pastry for 15 minutes, then remove the baking beans and parchment and bake for a further 5 minutes.

Meanwhile, make the filling. Cook the macaroni in plenty of salted water according to the packet instructions. Drain, then tip the macaroni back into the pan and put the lid on – the steam will help prevent the pasta from drying out.

Heat the butter in a large saucepan and add the onion. Sauté until the onion is soft and translucent, then turn up the heat and add the bacon. Continue to cook until the bacon has crisped up, then add the garlic and herbs and cook for another couple of minutes.

Sprinkle in the flour, mustard powder and curry powder, if using, and stir to make a paste around the onion and bacon. Gradually add the milk, stirring vigorously in between each addition, until you have incorporated it all and you have a sauce the texture of double cream. Add the cheeses and the chilli flakes, then stir until the cheeses have melted.

Add the macaroni to the sauce and stir until well combined. The sauce should be relatively loose around the macaroni – if it is too stiff and stodgy, add a little more milk. Stir in the tomatoes, if using.

Pour the sauce-coated macaroni into the pastry case, then mix the cheeses for the topping together and sprinkle them over the pie. Bake the pie for about 25 minutes until the top is bubbling and browned.

SPINACH & LENTIL PASTIES

We started this recipe as a sort of variation on spanakopita – the Greek spinach and filo pie – but then we experimented with a light and delicious rough puff pastry which really complements the filling and we came up with these little beauties. They're spot on we think and we bet you can't eat just one. You can, of course, use shop-bought puff, but this pastry is easy to make and well worth it.

Makes 8

Rough puff pastry
225g plain flour, plus extra
    for dusting
pinch of salt
225g butter, chilled and diced
    into 1cm cubes
125ml iced water

Filling
400g frozen spinach,
    defrosted
leaves from a small bunch
    of parsley, finely chopped
leaves from a small bunch
    of dill, finely chopped
leaves from a small bunch
    of mint, finely chopped
2 spring onions, finely chopped
1 garlic clove, grated or crushed
zest and juice of ½ lime
150g cooked brown, green
    or puy lentils (50g raw)
25g Parmesan, finely grated
    (optional)
1 tsp Baharat spice (optional)
1 egg, beaten, 1 tbsp
    reserved
salt and black pepper

First make the pastry – do this well in advance, as there is a lot of chilling time involved in this recipe.

Put the flour in a bowl with a pinch of salt. Add the butter and toss it so all the individual cubes are coated in flour. Rub or mash the cubes of butter so they flatten out – that's all you need to do. Don't rub them any smaller than that.

Pour in the water and briefly knead the mixture into a dough, handling it as little as possible. Put the dough in a container and chill it in the fridge for half an hour.

Dust your work surface with flour and roll the pastry out into a large rectangle measuring about 25 x 35–40cm. Cut it in half, widthways, then fold each rectangle twice so you end up with 4-layered rectangles. Wrap them or put them in a container and chill again for another hour.

For the filling, finely chop the spinach and squeeze as much liquid out of it as you can. Mix with all the remaining ingredients, including the Parmesan and Baharat spice, if using. Season with plenty of salt and pepper.

Remove one of the rectangles of pastry from the fridge. Dust your work surface with flour and roll the pastry out into a large square – measuring at least 30 x 30cm. Cut this into 4 smaller squares.

Pile filling into a triangle of each square (imagine the halfway line runs from corner to corner) – use about 50g of filling per pasty.

Mix the reserved egg with a tablespoon of water and use it to brush around the exposed edges of each square. Fold the uncovered pastry over the filling to make triangular parcels, then seal or crimp them well. Brush the top of the parcels with the reserved beaten egg.

Remove the remaining pastry from the fridge and repeat. Place the pasties on a couple of baking trays. Chill them for at least another 30 minutes, preferably an hour.

Preheat the oven to 200°C/Fan 180°C/Gas 6. Bake for 20–25 minutes, until the pastry is crisp and well browned. Good hot or cold.

DUTCH BABY

We discovered this strangely named dish in the States and basically it's a sort of cross between a pancake and a Yorkshire pudding. It can have a sweet or savoury filling and is baked in the oven. It's not difficult to make, but just be a bit careful about the size of the tomatoes – because of the length of time the baby needs to cook, larger cherry or plum cherry tomatoes work better than the tiny ones. Nice served with a courgette salad.

Serves 4

Filling

3 tbsp olive oil
3 medium red onions, finely sliced
2 garlic cloves, finely chopped
leaves from a thyme sprig
2 tsp sherry vinegar
300g plum cherry tomatoes or large cherry tomatoes
about 150g log-style goat's cheese (the sort with the rind)
1 tbsp olives, pitted and sliced (optional)
a few basil leaves
salt and black pepper

Batter

100g plain flour
1 tsp dried mixed herbs
4 eggs
175ml whole milk

Courgette salad (optional)

75g salad leaves
2 small to medium courgettes, very thinly sliced
a few thyme sprigs and basil leaves
2 tbsp olive oil
1 tsp sherry vinegar
zest and juice of ½ lemon

First start the filling. Heat 2 tablespoons of the oil in a frying pan and add the onions. Sauté over a low-medium heat until softened and starting to brown. Add the garlic and thyme, season with salt and pepper and continue to cook for a further 2 minutes. Stir in the sherry vinegar and cook for another minute. Remove the pan from the heat and leave to cool.

To make the batter, put the flour in a bowl with the dried herbs and a large pinch of salt. Beat in the eggs until you have a thick batter, then gradually whisk in the milk. You should end up with a smooth, slightly frothy batter with the consistency of unwhisked double cream. Set the batter aside to rest for about half an hour.

Preheat the oven to 200°C/Fan 180°C/Gas 6. Heat the remaining oil in a roasting tin on the hob. When the oil is smoking hot, pour in the batter and swirl it around so the base of the tin is completely coated. Sprinkle in the cooked onion mixture, then arrange the tomatoes and slices of cheese over the top – they will sink into the batter slightly. Add the olives, if using.

Bake in the preheated oven for 20–25 minutes, until the batter has puffed up around the cheese and tomatoes and the tomatoes are soft. They may burst, but that's fine.

Leave the dish to stand for 5 minutes – the baby will be easier to remove from the tin after resting.

To make the salad, if using, put the salad leaves and courgettes in a bowl with the herbs. Whisk the oil, vinegar and lemon zest and juice together and season with salt and pepper. Toss and serve.

LEEK & TOMATO TART

A touch of Mediterranean magic this one, using beautiful olive oil pastry. The tomatoes rest on a bed of leeks and anchovy paste to make a tart that's tantalisingly flavourful. Gorgeous with a simple side salad.

Serves 6–8

Pastry
250g plain flour (or 50/50
    wholemeal and white),
    plus extra for dusting
½ tsp baking powder
pinch of salt
75ml olive oil
1 egg, beaten
2–3 tbsp iced water

Filling
2 tbsp olive oil, plus more for
    brushing
4 leeks, thinly sliced into rounds
1 small onion, finely chopped
1 thyme sprig
2 garlic cloves, finely chopped
2 tbsp anchovy paste
1 tbsp capers, roughly chopped
zest of 1 lemon
up to 600g tomatoes (mix of
    cherry tomatoes and larger)
½ tsp dried oregano or herbes
    de Provence
salt and black pepper

For the pastry, put the flour in a bowl with the baking powder and a generous pinch of salt. Gradually work in the olive oil. Add the egg and just enough of the iced water to make a dough. Knead the dough very briefly until smooth, then turn it out on to a floured surface. Roll it out into a round to line a 25cm tart tin. Chill for at least half an hour.

Preheat the oven to 180°C/Fan 160°C/Gas 4. Prick the pastry base with a fork, then line the pastry with baking parchment and add some baking beans. Bake for about 15 minutes. Remove the beans and parchment, then put the pastry back in the oven for another 5–10 minutes until it's starting to take on some colour. Remove it from the oven and set aside.

To make the filling, heat the olive oil in a sauté pan and add the leeks and onion. Stir to coat them with the oil, then add the thyme. Season generously and add a splash of water – no more than 50ml. Cover and leave to braise until the leeks are tender – this will take at least 10–15 minutes. Add the garlic and cook for a further 2 minutes, then turn up the heat and cook until any liquid has evaporated off.

Spread the anchovy paste over the base of the tart case. Add the leek mixture, then sprinkle over the capers. Sprinkle the lemon zest over the top.

Halve any cherry tomatoes and slice any larger tomatoes to a similar thickness. Arrange them over the top of the leeks, leaving as few gaps as possible. Brush the tomatoes with olive oil and sprinkle with the oregano or herbes de Provence and a little salt.

Bake in the oven for 20–25 minutes until the tomatoes have softened and lightly browned. Best served at room temperature.

BAKED BEAN PIE

Who doesn't love a baked bean? This is the very definition of comfort food – beans, potatoes and cheese – and a real bear hug of a dish. The mustard just adds that little edge of heat, which is nice. Beans means pies!

Serves 4–6

750g potatoes, cut into
    1.5–2cm cubes
25g butter, plus extra for
    greasing
2 medium onions, thinly sliced
small bunch of parsley, finely
    chopped
800g baked beans (2 cans)
1 tbsp wholegrain mustard
100g Cheddar, grated
100g Gruyère or Comté cheese,
    grated
75g mozzarella, grated or torn
salt and black pepper

Put the potatoes in a steamer basket and steam them over simmering water for 8–10 minutes until tender.

Heat the butter in a frying pan and add the onions. Fry them over a medium heat until they are soft and translucent and starting to brown around the edges. Reserve a tablespoon of the parsley and stir the rest into the onions. Preheat the oven to 200°C/Fan 180°C/Gas 6.

Butter a deep ovenproof dish and add the onions and baked beans. Season with black pepper and stir to combine.

Put the steamed potatoes in a bowl. Stir in the mustard and season with salt and pepper. Stir in 75g each of the Cheddar and the Gruyère or Comté, then spoon the potato mixture over the baked beans. Mix the remaining cheese, including the mozzarella, with the reserved parsley and sprinkle over the top.

Bake in the oven for 25–30 minutes until the cheese has melted and browned and the baked beans are bubbling up under the potatoes.

BROWN SHRIMP SOUFFLÉS

We love brown shrimps and their intense flavour is just right here. These soufflés are dead impressive and are easier to make than you think – so don't be scared. We've gone with the twice-baked method, which means you can get the soufflés all ready, then reheat them when you want to eat. Don't miss out on the sauce – it finishes the dish off beautifully.

Makes 4

Ramekins
butter, for greasing
5g Parmesan, finely grated

Infused milk

200ml whole milk
1 slice of onion
a few peppercorns
a piece of pared lemon zest
1 mace blade

Soufflés

35g butter
35g plain flour
½ tsp mustard powder
½ tsp sweet paprika
¼ tsp cayenne
15g Parmesan, finely grated
1 tbsp tomato purée
3 eggs, separated
100g brown shrimp, chopped
1 tbsp lemon juice
¼ tsp cream of tartar
salt and black pepper

To twice bake

butter
10g Parmesan, finely grated

Sauce

15g olive oil
25g capers
25g butter
1 tsp tarragon mustard
zest and juice of 1 lemon
a few chives

Butter the insides of 4 x 150ml ramekins generously and sprinkle them with Parmesan, making sure the base and sides are completely covered. Chill the ramekins in the fridge.

Put the milk and all the aromatics in a pan and heat to just below boiling point. Leave the milk to infuse for half an hour, then strain and discard the aromatics.

Melt the butter in a saucepan. Add the flour, mustard powder, paprika and cayenne and stir until you have a thick, ochre-coloured paste. Gradually whisk in the infused milk – the mixture will get quite runny, then thicken to a béchamel sauce with the texture of thick custard. Remove the pan from the heat and season the sauce with salt and pepper. Tip the béchamel into a large bowl, stir in the Parmesan cheese and tomato purée and leave to cool. You can prepare ahead to this stage and chill the béchamel if necessary.

Beat the egg yolks into the bowl of béchamel. Toss the brown shrimp in the lemon juice and season with salt and pepper, then fold them into the sauce.

Preheat the oven to 180°C/Fan 160°C/Gas 4. Boil a kettle of water.

Put the egg whites in a bowl with the cream of tartar and whisk to the stiff peaks stage. Fold a large spoon of the egg whites into the shrimp mixture to loosen it a bit, then add the rest, folding it in with a metal spoon until there are no white streaks. Try to make sure you don't knock out too much air.

Pile the mixture into the prepared ramekins, right to the top. Take a palette knife across to the top to get a clean line, then run your finger around the rim. This will help the soufflés rise evenly.

Place the ramekins in a roasting tin and put the tin in the oven. Pull out the oven shelf slightly and pour enough freshly boiled water into the tin to come halfway up the sides of the ramekins. Bake the soufflés for 18–20 minutes until well risen and browned. Remove them from the oven and leave to cool – they will deflate to the top of the ramekins. You can prepare ahead to this stage and keep the soufflés in the fridge until you need them.

When you are ready to serve the soufflés, preheat the oven to 200°C/Fan 180°C/Gas 6. Butter a medium-sized ovenproof dish. Carefully run a palette knife around the edge of the ramekins, turn the soufflés out and place them in the dish. Sprinkle them with the Parmesan and bake in the oven for 10 minutes until piping hot.

To make the sauce, heat the oil in a frying pan until hot. Add the capers and fry them for a minute – they should sizzle. Whisk in the butter, followed by the mustard and finally the lemon zest and juice. Taste for seasoning and add a little salt and pepper if necessary. Spoon the sauce around the soufflés and garnish with some freshly snipped chives.

CRAB, COURGETTE & SAFFRON TART

A beautifully luxurious tart for a special treat. Makes a little crab meat go a long way.

Serves 6–8

Pastry
250g plain flour, plus extra
   for dusting
125g butter, chilled and diced
pinch of salt
1 egg
iced water

Filling
2 medium courgettes,
   coarsely grated
300ml double cream
large pinch of saffron
1 tbsp olive oil
1 garlic clove, finely chopped
zest of 1 lemon
3 eggs
100g brown crab meat
leaves from a large tarragon
   sprig, finely chopped
a few basil leaves, shredded
100g white crab meat
juice of ½ lemon
rasp of nutmeg (optional)
salt and black pepper

To serve
lemon wedges

First make the pastry case. Put the flour in a bowl and add the butter and a generous pinch of salt. Rub the butter into the flour until the mixture resembles fine breadcrumbs, then add the egg and just enough iced water to bring the dough together. Make sure it isn't too floury or the pastry will be crumbly and harder to roll.

Lightly flour your work surface and roll out the dough to fit a 25cm diameter fluted tart tin. Chill the pastry in the fridge for at least half an hour or in the freezer for 10–15 minutes.

Preheat the oven to 200°C/Fan 180°C/Gas 6. Line the pastry with baking parchment and add some baking beans. Bake in the oven for 15 minutes, then remove the baking beans and parchment and bake for a further 5 minutes until the pastry is completely set and starting to colour. Remove from the oven and leave to cool. Turn the oven down to 170°C/Fan 150°C/Gas 3½.

Sprinkle the courgettes with salt and leave them in a colander set over a bowl for half an hour – this helps draw out the moisture. Gently squeeze the courgettes in a tea towel to remove any remaining moisture.

Meanwhile, put 100ml of the cream in a small pan with the saffron. Heat gently, almost to boiling point, then remove from the heat and leave to cool.

Heat the oil in a frying pan and add the courgettes. Fry them for a few minutes over a gentle heat until they collapse a bit, then season with salt and pepper. Stir in the garlic and cook for a further minute, then add some of the lemon zest. Remove the pan from the heat and leave to cool.

Beat the eggs in a bowl until completely smooth, then stir in the saffron-infused cream, the rest of the cream, the brown crab meat and the herbs. Season with salt and pepper.

Put the pastry case in its tin on a baking tray. Spread the courgettes over the base of the pastry, then carefully pour in the custard mixture. Toss the white crab meat in the lemon juice, add a rasp of nutmeg, if using, and sprinkle it over the top of the custard. It will sink, but that's OK. Finish with a little more lemon zest.

Bake the tart in the oven for 30–35 minutes until the custard has just set – a bit of a wobble is good. Remove it from the oven and leave to stand for 10–15 minutes. Serve warm or at room temperature with a tomato salad and lemon wedges on the side. Small portions make a lovely starter too.

CURRIED CHICKEN PIE

You can't beat a chicken pie. We fancied going with an Indian vibe with this one, so we've added some spice to the filling and some turmeric to the pastry. And you know how everyone loves a dollop of mango chutney with a curry? We've suggested spreading the pastry with chutney before you add the filling to get a blast of that lovely flavour.

Serves 6

100ml thick yoghurt
juice of 1 lemon
1 tbsp medium curry powder
800g skinless, boneless
   chicken thigh or breast
   fillets, diced
1 large onion, roughly chopped
15g root ginger, peeled and
   roughly chopped
4 garlic cloves, roughly chopped
1 tbsp vegetable or coconut oil
1 tsp mustard seeds
1 tsp turmeric
1 tbsp tomato purée
450g spinach
30g ground almonds
small bunch of coriander,
   finely chopped
salt and black pepper

Pastry

300g plain flour, plus extra
   for dusting
½ tsp turmeric
150g butter, chilled and diced
2–3 tbsp iced water

To assemble

3–4 tbsp mango chutney
   (optional)
1 egg, beaten, for brushing

First make the filling. Put the yoghurt, lemon juice and curry powder in a bowl and add a teaspoon of salt and plenty of black pepper. Add the chicken and stir so everything is thoroughly combined. Cover and leave to marinate for about half an hour – any longer and it's best to put it in the fridge.

Put the onion, ginger and garlic into a food processor and blitz to a paste. Heat the oil in a large flameproof casserole dish and add the mustard seeds. When they pop, add the onion paste and stir for several minutes until the mixture starts to colour. Stir in the turmeric and tomato purée.

Continue to cook for a few minutes until the paste starts to separate, then add the chicken – including all the marinade – to the pan. Cook over a high heat, stirring regularly, for several minutes, then turn down the heat to a simmer and leave to cook gently for about 20 minutes. During this time the chicken will cook through and the sauce will reduce – aim for something the texture of double cream.

While the chicken is cooking, wash the spinach well, put it into a saucepan and place it over the heat until wilted down. Drain it thoroughly, then chop and squeeze out any excess moisture.

Stir the almonds into the chicken, followed by the spinach and the coriander. Taste for seasoning and spice, then remove from the heat and leave to cool.

To make the pastry, mix together the flour, turmeric and half a teaspoon of salt in a bowl. Rub in the butter, then add just enough iced water to mix to a smooth dough.

Divide the pastry into two-thirds and one-third. Take the larger piece and roll it out on a floured work surface. Use it to line a pie dish – an ordinary round metal one, measuring about 5cm deep and 21cm across, is best. Put it in the fridge to chill, then wrap the remaining pastry and chill that too.

Preheat the oven to 200°C/Fan 180°C/Gas 6. Spread the mango chutney, if using, over the pastry, then add the filling. Roll out the remaining pastry and place it over the filling. Seal the edges with beaten egg and crimp together. Brush the pie with more egg.

Bake the pie in the oven for about 30 minutes until it is golden brown around the edges and piping hot inside. Nice with a salad or some green veg.

CHICKEN & TARRAGON PASTIES

From Cornwall to Canterbury, these pasties are brilliant. If you like, you can also make them with cooked turkey, so a great way of using up Christmas leftovers. You'd need about 500g of meat and some chicken or turkey stock instead of the cooking liquor for the sauce.

Makes 8

Filling

750g skinless, boneless
    chicken thigh or breast fillets
2 bay leaves
1 large tarragon sprig
100ml white wine
1 tbsp olive oil
250g mushrooms, roughly
    chopped
leaves from 1 tarragon sprig,
    finely chopped
2 garlic cloves, finely chopped
1 egg, beaten, for brushing
salt and black pepper

Sauce

50g butter
1 leek, finely chopped
50g plain flour
300ml cooking liquor
1 tbsp tarragon mustard
1 tarragon sprig, finely chopped
50ml double cream

Pastry

450g plain flour
2 tsp baking powder
½ tsp salt
150g butter, chilled and diced
1 egg, beaten
iced water

First make the filling, as it needs time to cool down and chill before using. Put the chicken in a lidded sauté pan and season with salt and pepper. Add the bay leaves and tarragon sprig, then pour over the white wine and just enough water to cover – you'll need about 500ml. Bring to the boil, then turn the heat down, cover the pan and simmer for 5 minutes.

Remove the pan from the heat and set it aside until the chicken has cooled to room temperature. Strain the liquid into a jug and measure 300ml of it for use in the sauce. Save the rest to use as a light chicken stock another time.

Dice the chicken. Heat the olive oil in a frying pan and add the mushrooms and season with salt and pepper. Fry them over a high heat until they have given out their liquid and the pan is starting to look dry. Add the tarragon and garlic and cook for a further couple of minutes.

For the sauce, heat the butter in a saucepan and add the chopped leek. Stir until the leek looks glossy with butter, then put a lid on the pan and leave over a very low heat for a few minutes until the leek is tender.

Stir in the flour until you have a leek-flecked roux, then gradually add the reserved cooking liquor, whisking as you go, to make a thick sauce. Whisk in the mustard and chopped tarragon, followed by the cream, then remove the pan from the heat. Stir in the chicken and mushrooms, then leave to cool. When the mixture is at room temperature, put it in the fridge to chill for at least half an hour.

To make the pastry, put the flour and baking powder in a bowl and add the salt. Add the butter and rub it in until the mixture resembles fine breadcrumbs. Add the egg and just enough water to bring the pastry together to form a firm dough – make sure it isn't at all dry and flaky or it will be harder to work with. Chill for half an hour.

To assemble the pasties, divide the pastry and the filling into 8 portions of each – the easiest way to do this is by weight. Roll out each piece of pastry into a round measuring about 19–20cm. Put a portion of the filling on one half of a round. Brush the edges with beaten egg, then fold the uncovered pastry over the filling. Seal the edges and crimp. Repeat with the remaining pastry and filling.

Preheat the oven to 200°C/Fan 180°C/Gas 6. Arrange the pasties on a large baking tray, then brush them thoroughly with beaten egg. Bake in the oven for about 30 minutes until golden brown and piping hot. Serve hot or cold.

CORNED BEEF HASH GALETTE

We do love a corned beef hash and a hash in a pie is bang on! A galette is just a fancy name for an open free-form pie and to make it even quicker to put together, you could use shop-bought puff pastry. We do recommend adding the cheesy topping – yum.

Serves 4–6

Pastry
250g plain flour
pinch of salt
65g butter, chilled and diced
60g lard (or another 60g
    butter), chilled and diced
1 egg, beaten

Filling

125g swede, diced
125g potato, diced
1 large carrot, diced
1 tbsp olive oil
1 large onion, finely chopped
250g corned beef, diced
2 garlic cloves, finely chopped
leaves from 1 thyme sprig
2 tsp Dijon mustard
2 tbsp tomato ketchup
a good dash of
    Worcestershire sauce
salt and black pepper

Topping (optional)

35g Cheddar or other hard
    cheese, grated
a few parsley leaves, finely
    chopped

First make the pastry. Put the flour in a bowl with a generous pinch of salt. Add the butter and the lard, if using, then rub it into the flour until the mixture resembles fine breadcrumbs. Add all but a tablespoon of the egg and just enough cold water to bind the dough together. Make sure the dough isn't crumbly, as you will be making a free-form tart and it will be harder to patch together. Chill the pastry until you are ready to roll it.

To make the filling, put the swede, potato and carrot into a saucepan and add salt. Cover with cold water and bring to the boil. Simmer until the vegetables are just tender – this shouldn't take more than 3–4 minutes because of their size. Drain and leave to cool.

Heat the olive oil in a frying pan. Add the onion and sauté over a medium-high heat until softened and slightly caramelised around the edges. Add the corned beef, garlic and thyme and cook for another couple of minutes. Stir in the mustard, ketchup and Worcestershire sauce and season with salt and pepper. Add this to the vegetables and stir well. Leave to cool.

Preheat the oven to 200°C/Fan 180°C/Gas 6. Roll out the pastry into a large round. Carefully place this on a large baking tray – it might overlap the edges of the tray, but that's fine. Pile the filling on to the pastry, leaving a 3–4cm border all around. Fold the pastry border over the filling, leaving much of the filling exposed.

If including the topping, mix the cheese with the parsley and sprinkle over the exposed filling.

Add a little water to the reserved tablespoon of beaten egg and use the mixture to brush the pastry. Bake the galette in the preheated oven for 25–30 minutes until the pastry is golden. Serve piping hot.

STEAK BAKES

These are epic, we promise you – a home-made version of the hangover favourite from that popular high-street baker. The really important thing is to let the filling cool down properly before adding it to the pastry or it will make the pastry go all soggy and the sauce will run all over the place. All you need to do is to get a bit organised and make the filling well in advance so it has time to chill. Then put your little parcels of bliss together, bake and enjoy! These are so good, it might be worth making a double quantity of the filling and freezing the rest for another time.

Makes 4

2 tbsp olive oil or dripping
400g stewing or braising steak, finely chopped
1 onion, finely chopped
2 garlic cloves, finely chopped
1 heaped tbsp plain flour
1 tsp mustard powder
1 tsp tomato purée
100g red wine
200ml beef stock
1 thyme sprig
1 x 320g pack of ready-rolled, puff pastry
flour, for dusting
1 egg, beaten
salt and black pepper

First make the filling. Heat half the oil or dripping in a frying pan. Season the steak with salt and pepper, then add it to the pan. Fry it over a high heat until seared on all sides, then remove and set aside.

Heat the remaining oil or dripping in a saucepan. Add the onion and sauté it until soft and translucent. Add the garlic and cook for a further couple of minutes, then stir in the flour and mustard powder. Cook for another couple of minutes, stirring constantly, then stir in the tomato purée.

Pour in the red wine. Allow it to bubble up and reduce down, then add the beef stock and thyme. Season with salt again, then put the beef in the pan.

Bring back to the boil, then turn the heat down to a simmer and cover the pan. Leave to cook for 45 minutes to an hour until the beef is tender. Remove the pan from the heat and leave the filling to cool down. Once it is cool, put it in the fridge and chill for at least an hour.

When you are ready to assemble and cook the pies, preheat the oven to 200°C/Fan 180°C/Gas 6 and line a baking tray with baking parchment.

Take the puff pastry and unroll it on a lightly floured work surface. Cut the pastry in half lengthways, then cut each half into 4 equal rectangles so you have 8 pieces in total.

Take a quarter of the filling and place it on top of a piece of pastry, making sure you leave a border of 1cm all the way round. Brush the exposed edges with beaten egg, then take another piece of pastry and place it over the top. You may have to stretch it slightly but that's fine – puff pastry is very stretchy anyway. Make sure the edges are well sealed by crimping them with the prongs of a fork, then place the parcel on a baking tray. Brush thoroughly with beaten egg and cut a couple of small steam holes in the top.

Repeat with the remaining pastry and filling until you have 4 parcels. Bake in the oven for 20–25 minutes until puffed up, golden brown and piping hot.

ACCORDION BISCUITS WITH SAUSAGE GRAVY

These American-style biscuits are more like our scones and are mega good. Serve them with the sausage gravy and a big pile of greens or as a tasty addition to a full English.

Serves 4

Biscuits
300g plain flour, plus extra
    for dusting
1 tbsp baking powder
1 tbsp caster sugar (optional)
pinch of salt
125g butter, diced and chilled
75g cream cheese
125ml double cream
2 eggs, beaten,
    reserving 2 tbsp for brushing

Sausage gravy

1 tbsp olive oil
1 onion, finely chopped
200g sausage meat (squeezed
    from sausage casings)
large thyme sprig or
    ½ tsp dried thyme
25ml flour
500ml milk or 250ml milk
    and 250ml vegetable
    or chicken stock
dash of Worcestershire sauce
salt and black pepper

Put the flour and baking powder into a bowl and add the sugar, if using, and a good pinch of salt. Add the butter and rub it in quite roughly so the mixture has quite a coarse texture. To make sure the mixture stays cool, you could mash the butter in with a fork or cut it in with a pastry blender, rather than use your fingers. Put this in the freezer for 5 minutes, or in the fridge for 20.

Beat the cream cheese to loosen it up, then mix in the cream. Add the eggs, setting aside 2 tablespoonfuls for later, and stir until smooth.

Remove the bowl of flour and butter from the fridge or freezer and add the cream mixture. Keep the mixing to an absolute minimum as you bring everything together into a dough – it doesn't matter if it is still a bit floury.

Dust your work surface with flour. Turn the dough out and pat it into a rectangle measuring about 20 x 16cm. Cut the dough in half and place one half on top of the other. Repeat this same procedure twice more. When you pat the dough into a rectangle for the last time, aim for a height of 2.5–3cm.

Cut the dough into rounds using a 6.5cm cutter. Make sure your cutter is well dusted with flour and press it down without twisting. Squish together the offcuts and pat the dough down again before cutting out more rounds – you should get 8–10. Place the rounds on a baking tray. Chill them for another 10 minutes in the freezer or half an hour in the fridge.

When you are ready to bake your biscuits, preheat the oven to 200°C/Fan 180°C/Gas 6. Brush the biscuits with the reserved beaten egg and bake them for 20–25 minutes until well risen and golden on top.

To make the sausage gravy, heat the olive oil in a deep frying pan or sauté pan and add the onion. Sauté until soft and translucent. Turn the heat up to medium and add the sausage meat. Break it up with the back of a wooden spoon and fry until lightly browned. You should notice some fat rendering out of the sausage meat. Season with salt and pepper.

Add the thyme and sprinkle in the flour. Stir until the flour forms a thick paste around the onion and sausage meat and make sure you scrape up any brown bits on the base of the pan too. Start adding the milk, followed by the stock, if using, a little at a time, to make a sauce with the consistency of pourable double cream. Add the Worcestershire sauce.

If your gravy is too thick, add a little water or more stock. Bring to the boil, then simmer until ready to serve. If reheating just before serving, make sure you give the gravy a good whisk beforehand. Serve with the biscuits.

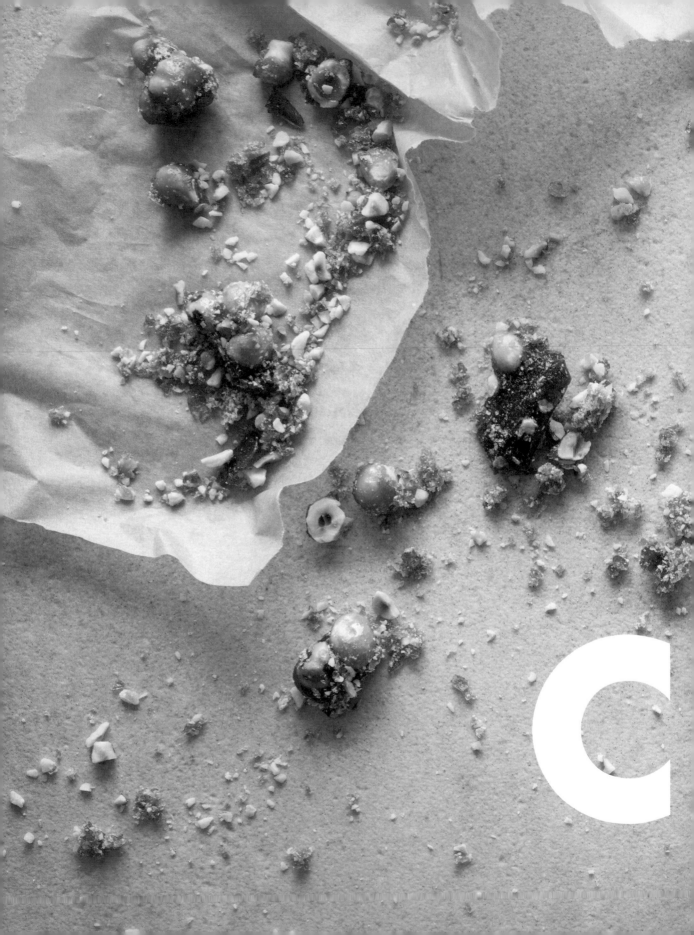

AKES

LIME & COCONUT DRIZZLE CAKE

In our updated version of the ever-popular lemon drizzle cake, we've gone a bit beyond and used zingy lime and a dash of tequila too, if you fancy. Really tasty, we think, and the coconut adds a lovely bit of extra texture.

Makes 10–12 slices

175g butter, softened, plus
    extra for greasing
175g caster sugar
zest of 3–4 limes
    (depending on size)
pinch of salt
200g self-raising flour
50g desiccated coconut
½ tsp baking powder
3 eggs
3–4 tbsp milk

Syrup

150g icing sugar
juice of 3–4 limes
    (depending on size)
2–3 tsp tequila, to taste
    (optional)

Preheat the oven to 180°C/Fan 160°C/Gas 4. Grease a large (900g) loaf tin and line it with baking parchment.

Using electric beaters, beat the butter and caster sugar with the lime zest and a pinch of salt until very soft and fluffy.

Mix the flour, coconut and baking powder together in a bowl. Add one of the eggs to the butter mixture, followed by a heaped tablespoon of the flour. Mix and repeat until you have used all the eggs, then fold in the rest of the flour. Add just enough milk to make a mixture with a dropping consistency.

Scrape the mixture into the prepared tin and bake for 35–40 minutes, until well risen and golden brown. The cake may crack down the centre but this is all part of its charm. Remove the cake from the oven, but leave it in the tin.

For the syrup, put the icing sugar and lime juice into a saucepan and heat gently until the sugar has dissolved. Add the tequila, if using.

While the cake is still warm from the oven, pierce it all over with a skewer and pour over the hot syrup. Leave it to cool completely before slicing. Delicious on its own or with a dollop of cream.

CHOCOLATE GINGERBREAD

This one requires a little self-discipline. While many cakes are best eaten on the day they are baked, gingerbread improves with time. Wrap these up, stash them away in a tin and enjoy a lovely sticky treat a few days later. It's worth the wait, we promise.

Makes 16 squares

250g plain flour
50g cocoa powder
2 tbsp ground ginger
1 tsp ground cinnamon
¼ tsp cayenne or hot chilli
   powder
pinch of salt
150g butter
125g dark brown soft sugar
200g golden syrup
200g black treacle
150ml whole milk
1 heaped tsp bicarbonate
   of soda
2 eggs
50g dark chocolate,
   finely chopped

Preheat the oven to 170°C/Fan 150°C/Gas 3½. Line a 30 x 20cm baking tin with baking parchment.

Sift the flour into a large bowl with the cocoa and spices. Add a generous pinch of salt and stir or whisk to combine.

Put the butter, sugar, golden syrup and treacle into a saucepan. Heat gently until everything has melted together.

Remove the pan from the heat and whisk in the milk, bicarbonate of soda and eggs. Don't be surprised if the mixture froths up a little.

Gradually stir the contents of the saucepan into the flour mixture, making sure it's all well combined and there are no little pockets of flour. You should have a very wet, pourable batter. Stir in the chocolate.

Pour the batter into the prepared tin and bake in the oven for 45–50 minutes. When the edges of the gingerbread have pulled back slightly from the side of tin and it's springy to the touch, it's done.

Leave the gingerbread to cool in the tin for half an hour, then remove it and place it on a wire rack to cool completely before cutting it into squares. If possible, wrap the cake and keep it for several days before eating – this will allow it to develop the classic gingerbread stickiness as it matures.

SWEDISH APPLE CAKE

We've created a belter here – a classic apple cake with the traditional Swedish flavours of cardamom and cinnamon. This is a simple bake with a lovely mix of textures. It's really delicious at teatime with a cuppa or as a dessert with some cream or custard.

Makes about 15 slices

175g butter, melted, plus extra
    for greasing
200g plain flour
100g wholemeal flour
1½ tsp baking powder
½ tsp ground cardamom
½ tsp ground cinnamon
pinch of salt
4 eggs
225g light brown soft sugar
50ml milk

Apples

3 eating apples, peeled, cored
    and cut into slim wedges
2 tbsp demerara sugar
½ tsp ground cardamom
½ tsp ground cinnamon

To finish

2 tbsp apple or apricot jam,
    for glazing

Preheat the oven to 180°C/Fan 160°C/Gas 4. Grease a 30 x 20cm rectangular baking tin and line it with baking parchment.

Put both flours in a bowl with the baking powder, spices and a pinch of salt, then stir to combine.

Put the eggs and sugar in a separate bowl and whisk until the mixture is very thick and frothy – almost mousse-like. This will take a while and is best done with electric beaters.

Pour the milk into the melted butter and whisk together lightly. Fold this mixture into the eggs and sugar, then add the flour. Fold in the flour until you have a smooth, runny batter with no streaks. Pour the batter into the prepared tin.

Put the apples in a bowl, sprinkle over the sugar and spices and mix well. Don't be tempted to do this in advance, as you don't want the apples to give out liquid. Arrange the apples over the top of the batter, then bake the cake in the oven for 30–35 minutes until it's golden-brown and springy to touch.

Melt the apple or apricot jam in a small saucepan and brush it over the cake while it's still warm. Leave the cake to cool in the tin, then cut it into slices. Store in an airtight tin.

HUMMINGBIRD CAKE

This is an impressive cake and good for a celebration, but it's not hard to make. The pineapple and banana make for a lovely moist texture, and it's all topped off with a delicious cream cheese icing. They'll be queuing up for slices of this.

Makes 8–12 slices

250g self-raising flour
½ tsp baking powder
½ tsp ground cinnamon
¼ tsp ground cloves
rasp of nutmeg
pinch of salt
3 eggs
150g light brown soft sugar
1 tsp vanilla extract
zest of 1 lime
175ml sunflower oil
3 bananas, mashed
150g pineapple, finely chopped
(canned is fine)
50g walnuts or pecans, finely
chopped

Cream cheese icing

100g butter, softened
pinch of salt
150g icing sugar
a few drops of vanilla extract
or zest of 1 lime
200g cream cheese

To garnish (optional)

50g walnuts or pecans,
very finely chopped

Preheat the oven to 180°C/Fan 160°C/Gas 4. Line 2 x 20–21cm diameter sandwich tins with baking parchment.

Put the flour, baking powder and spices into a bowl with a generous pinch of salt and whisk briefly to combine and get rid of any lumps.

Put the eggs, sugar, vanilla extract and lime zest into a bowl and whisk until really well aerated. Beat in the sunflower oil, then fold in the flour mixture, mashed bananas, chopped pineapple and nuts. Divide the mixture evenly between the tins – weigh the mixture if you want precision and a very even bake – and smooth it down.

Bake the cakes in the preheated oven for 25–30 minutes until the sponge is a good colour and well risen. It should also have shrunk slightly away from the sides of the tin. Leave the cakes in the tins to cool.

For the icing, put the butter in a bowl with a pinch of salt and beat until soft and pale. Gradually add in the icing sugar, a couple of tablespoons at a time, until the mixture is soft and well aerated. Add the vanilla extract or lime zest, then beat in the cream cheese. Keep the mixing to a minimum at this stage but make sure the icing is nice and smooth. You are aiming for a reluctant dropping consistency, but on a hot day it might be runnier. Leave the icing to chill in the fridge for at least an hour until it has firmed up a little and is a spreadable consistency.

When you are ready to put everything together, spread about a third of the icing over one of the cakes, then top with the remaining cake. Spread a thick layer of icing on top of the cake, then use any remaining icing on the sides, working from the bottom up with a metal spatula and applying it quite thinly. Smooth the top of the cake down and sprinkle with the nuts, if using.

SPICED HONEY CAKE

This is similar to the lovely French cake known as pain d'epices, which, by the way, the French like to serve with savoury goodies, such as pâté. There's no butter or oil in it, just some buttermilk, and it has a nice spicy flavour. Do try to leave this cake for a few days before eating it, as it gets even more delicious with time.

Makes 10–12 slices

350g runny honey
50g dark brown soft sugar
125g plain flour
125g dark rye flour
2 tsp baking powder
½ tsp bicarbonate of soda
2 tsp mixed spice
½ tsp ground cinnamon
½ tsp each of anise seeds,
   fennel seeds and caraway
   seeds
pinch of salt
100ml buttermilk
2 eggs, beaten

Preheat the oven to 170°C/Fan 150°C/Gas 3½. Line a large (900g) loaf tin with baking parchment.

Put the honey and sugar in a saucepan and heat gently until the honey has become more liquid and the sugar has dissolved. Remove the pan from the heat and leave to cool for a few minutes.

Put the plain flour and rye flour in a bowl with the baking powder, bicarb, spices, seeds and a generous pinch of salt, then stir.

Stir the buttermilk and eggs into the cooled honey mixture, then pour this into the dry ingredients. Combine, keeping mixing to a minimum. Pour the batter into the prepared tin.

Bake the cake in the oven for 40–45 minutes until well risen and a skewer comes out clean. Leave it to cool in the tin, then wrap it in foil and do your best to leave it alone for at least a couple of days before eating it. Enjoy it sliced, warmed through or toasted, with butter.

CHERRY MADEIRA CAKE

We both have fond memories of madeira cake from our childhoods – both our mams used to make it and it was a regular feature on the tea table – the go-to northern cake. For our latest recipe, we've jazzed things up a bit by adding cherries, which make it extra delicious, but you can leave the cake plain if you prefer.

Makes about 8 slices

175g butter, softened, plus
    extra for greasing
175g self-raising flour
75 g ground almonds
    or plain flour
pinch of salt
175g golden caster sugar
zest of 1 lemon (optional)
3 eggs
2–3 tbsp milk

Cherries

200g glacé cherries
1 tbsp plain flour or ground
    almonds

Preheat the oven to 180°C/Fan 160°C/Gas 4. Butter and line an 18cm round tin or a small loaf tin with baking parchment.

Cut the cherries into 2–3 pieces each, then rinse them if they're very sticky from the syrup (the ones at the bottom of the pot are usually sitting in thick syrup). Leave them to dry on kitchen paper or a clean tea towel while you make the cake batter.

Mix the self-raising flour with the ground almonds or plain flour and a generous pinch of salt.

Beat the butter and sugar together in a bowl with the lemon zest, if using, until softened and well combined. Add the eggs, one at a time, with a couple of tablespoons of the flour mix each time. Fold in the rest of the flour and just enough milk to give the batter a reluctant dropping consistency. Dust the cherries with the flour or ground almonds, then fold them into the batter.

Scrape the batter into the prepared tin and bake the cake for 45 minutes to an hour until golden brown on top. A toothpick should come out virtually clean and the cake will have shrunk away from the sides of the tin very slightly.

Leave the cake to cool in the tin, then remove and store in an airtight container.

STRAWBERRIES & CREAM VICTORIA SPONGE

We doff our caps to the WI for this one – they know what makes a good Victoria sponge. Their time-honoured method is to weigh the eggs in their shells, then use the same quantity of flour, sugar and butter. Never fails. We love filling our cake with strawberries and clotted cream which is so fresh and tasty and makes a good dessert, but feel free to use strawberry jam and whipped double cream if you prefer.

Makes 8–12 slices

butter, softened (see method)
4 medium or 3 large eggs
self-raising flour (see method)
2 tsp baking powder
pinch of salt
caster sugar (see method)
½ tsp vanilla extract
2–3 tbsp milk

Filling

250g strawberries, hulled
   and roughly chopped
squeeze of lemon juice
pinch of salt
2 tsp icing sugar
2–3 tbsp strawberry jam
1 x 113g pot of clotted cream

Preheat the oven to 180°C/Fan 160°C/Gas 4. Butter 2 x 20cm sandwich tins and line them with rounds of baking parchment.

Weigh the eggs in their shells. Measure out the same quantity of flour and mix in the baking powder and a generous pinch of salt. Measure the same amount of butter and sugar. You'll need a little extra caster sugar for dusting the top of the cake.

Cream the butter and sugar together until very soft and aerated. Add the eggs, one at a time, with a heaped tablespoon of the flour mixture each time, then fold them into the butter and sugar mixture until thoroughly combined. Fold in any remaining flour. Add the vanilla extract and just enough milk to give the mixture a dropping consistency.

Divide the mixture evenly between the tins. You can weigh the amount if you want to be absolutely sure your layers will be the same thickness. Bake the cakes in the oven for about 25 minutes until they are well risen, springy to touch and have slightly shrunk away from the sides of the tin. Turn the cakes out on to a wire rack and leave to cool completely.

To make the filling, put the strawberries in a bowl and squeeze over a little lemon juice. Add a pinch of salt and the icing sugar and stir until the sugar has dissolved. Leave to stand for half an hour.

Spread jam over the top of one of the sponges. Stir the cream to soften it up a little, then spread half of it over the jam. Strain the strawberries and arrange them on top. Spread the rest of the cream over the base of the remaining sponge and place it, cream-side down, on top of the other sponge. Dust the top with caster sugar.

Serve on the day and keep any leftovers in the fridge for up to 2 days.

If you're in full-on celebratory mode and want to make a three-tier cake, use an extra egg and adjust the rest of the ingredients accordingly. And when it's not strawberry season, try using blackberries, raspberries, blueberries or whatever takes your fancy.

BEE STING CAKE

This is a traditional German cake and is much loved. It's made with a yeasted dough, filled with buttercream, then topped with a honey drizzle and slices of stem ginger. The name refers to the contribution of the honey bee, spiced up with the tangy ginger.

Makes about 12 slices

Dough
250g plain flour, plus extra
  for dusting
1½ tsp fast-acting yeast
½ tsp salt
1 tbsp runny honey
60ml tepid milk
2 eggs
85g softened butter

Topping
75ml runny honey
2 balls of stem ginger,
  very finely sliced
½ tsp ground cinnamon
1–2 tsp whisky, bourbon or rum
  (to taste)
1 portion of candied lime zest
  (see p.270)

Honey and ginger
buttercream
125g butter, softened
250g icing sugar, well sifted
2 tbsp honey
2 tbsp ginger syrup (from the jar
  of stem ginger)
2 balls of stem ginger, finely
  chopped (optional)
1–2 tsp whisky, bourbon or rum
  (optional)

First make the dough. Put the flour into a bowl and add the yeast. Stir well, then add the salt.

Add the honey to the milk and stir to dissolve, then beat in the eggs. Add the wet ingredients to the dry to make a very sticky dough. Gradually add the butter, a teaspoon at a time until it is completely incorporated.

Turn the dough out on to a floured surface and knead until the stickiness has gone and the dough is smooth. It should also pass the windowpane test. To do this, break off a small piece of dough and stretch it out until it is so thin you can almost see through it. If you can do this, the gluten has developed enough and the dough is ready. If the dough breaks, knead for longer.

Cover the dough with a damp tea towel and leave it to rise for an hour to an hour and a half. It won't quite double in size, but it should be springy and well aerated. Knock it back and put it into a 23cm round loose-bottomed tin. Cover again and leave to prove for another 40–45 minutes. It should rise again until springy to touch. Preheat the oven to 180°C/Fan 160°C/Gas 4.

Bake the cake for 25–30 minutes until well risen and a rich golden brown. Meanwhile, make the topping. Put the honey into a small pan and place it over a gentle heat until melted. Add the stem ginger, cinnamon and whisky, bourbon or rum.

Remove the cake from the oven. While it is still warm, drizzle over the honey and ginger mixture, making sure you spread out the slices of ginger. Leave to cool in the tin.

For the buttercream, beat the butter and icing sugar together until very soft, light and fluffy, then beat in the honey and ginger syrup. Add the stem ginger and the alcohol, if using. If the texture is very dense, add up to a tablespoon of hot water so the mixture is just about dropping consistency.

When the cake is completely cool, remove it from the tin and place it on a flat surface. Carefully slice it in half horizontally and remove the top (don't turn it over or some of the ginger will fall off). Pipe or spread the buttercream over the base of the cake. Replace the top of the cake, then decorate it with the candied lime zest.

ST CLEMENT'S BATTENBERG

This is one our finest creations and is based on an orange and lemon Victoria sponge we made years ago. It's much easier than it looks – basically you just have to make two lovely cakes and stack them together. Don't worry if you don't end up with exact squares – it tastes just as good with rectangles or uneven pieces. If you're feeling flush and want to save a bit of time, you can buy a special Battenberg tin.

Makes 9–12 slices

Lemon sponge

75g self-raising flour
25g ground almonds
½ tsp baking powder
pinch of salt
100g butter, softened
100g caster sugar
zest of 2 lemons and
   2 tbsp lemon juice
a few drops of yellow
   food colouring
2 eggs

Orange sponge

75g self-raising flour
25g ground almonds
½ tsp baking powder
pinch of salt
100g butter, softened
100g caster sugar
zest of 2 oranges and
   2 tbsp orange juice
a few drops of orange
   food colouring
2 eggs

To assemble

icing sugar, for dusting
300g white marzipan
   (shop-bought or see p.267)
lemon curd or apricot jam

You'll need a 20cm square tin. Cut a strip of foil the same width as the tin and long enough to cover the base and 2 sides and to make a dividing wall down the middle of the tin. Fold a pleat in the middle of the foil and tuck a firm piece of cardboard into it – this will make the wall between your sponges. Butter the tin and carefully press the foil into the base of it, making sure the raised pleat 'wall' is exactly in the middle.

Make the lemon sponge. Mix the flour, ground almonds and baking powder together with a generous pinch of salt. Put the butter and sugar in a bowl with the zest and a few drops of colouring. Beat together for a couple of minutes until well combined and lightly aerated. At this point you should expect the colour to be quite intense – it will be muted once the remaining ingredients are added and again when it is baked. Bearing this in mind, add more colouring if necessary.

Add the eggs, one at a time with a couple of tablespoons of the flour mixture, then fold in the remaining flour and add just enough juice to give the mixture a reluctant dropping consistency.

Make the orange sponge in the same way. Preheat the oven to 180°C/Fan 160°C/Gas 4.

Scrape the 2 batters into their separate halves of the prepared tin, making sure the centre wall is as straight as possible. Bake in the preheated oven for about 25 minutes until the cakes are golden brown on top and springy to the touch. Remove from the oven and leave to cool in the tin. If you have time, chill the cakes for a few hours, preferably overnight, as this will make them much easier to cut and will give a cleaner result.

Remove the cakes from the tin and peel away the foil. Cut each cake in half lengthways, then trim the sides so they are perfectly straight – using a ruler will help. If you want your Battenberg to be a perfect square, trim to make sure the short sides are completely equal. Place the pieces on top of one another, contrasting the colours to form a checkerboard, and measure the length of the short sides. Set aside.

Dust your work surface with icing sugar and roll out the marzipan – the length should be just slightly longer than the length of your sponges and the width should be the length of the 4 short sides with a little overlap. Spread the long centre sides with lemon curd or apricot jam, then stick the cakes together.

Spread the underside with curd or jam and place the cake in the centre of the rolled-out marzipan. Spread more curd or jam on the 3 long exposed sides, then bring up the marzipan to cover. Smooth the marzipan so it is a tight fit around the sponges, then press the edges together, trimming off any overlap. Trim the marzipan and a thin layer of the sponge at each end of the Battenberg so it looks completely straight. Cut into slices to serve.

COFFEE & HAZELNUT CAKE

This three-tiered extravaganza is a real feast of a cake for a special occasion and it looks gorgeous. We've used a rather clever little icing that contains much less sugar than usual and has the taste and texture of fresh cream.

Makes 8–12 slices

Syrup
100g freshly brewed coffee
100g caster sugar
pinch of salt
25ml Frangelico liqueur
   (optional)

Hazelnut sponge

200g self-raising flour
125g hazelnuts, ground
½ tsp baking powder
pinch of salt
200g butter, softened
200g caster sugar
3 eggs
½ tsp vanilla extract
2 tbsp milk or Frangelico liqueur

Coffee icing

30g icing sugar
1 tbsp cornflour
1 tsp espresso powder
pinch of salt
500ml double or whipping
   cream, well chilled

Hazelnut praline (optional)

150g caster sugar
100g hazelnuts (preferably
   blanched)

To assemble

75–125g dark chocolate

For the syrup, put the coffee and sugar into a small saucepan with a pinch of salt. Slowly heat until the sugar has dissolved, then bring to the boil and simmer for 5 minutes or until the mixture starts to look syrupy. Remove from the heat and add the Frangelico, if using. Leave to cool.

Preheat the oven to 180°C/Fan 160°C/Gas 4. Line 3 x 20–21cm sandwich tins with some baking parchment. If you only have 2 tins, don't worry – bake 2 sponges, then bake another on its own.

Mix together the flour, hazelnuts and baking powder with a pinch of salt. Put the butter and sugar in a separate bowl and beat for a couple of minutes until soft and well combined. Add the eggs, one at a time with a couple of tablespoons of the flour mixture, beating well after each addition. Fold in the remaining flour, add the vanilla extract, then just enough milk or Frangelico to give a dropping consistency.

Divide the mixture between the tins and bake for 20–25 minutes until well risen and springy to touch. Remove the cakes from the oven and turn them out on to a cooling rack. Brush the base of each cake generously with some of the syrup while they are still warm.

For the icing, put the icing sugar, cornflour, espresso powder and a pinch of salt in a pan and whisk to combine. Gradually whisk in 125ml of the cream, then set the pan over a low heat and stir until smooth. Turn up the heat and stir constantly until the mixture thickens. Make sure it is lump-free by whisking furiously, then scrape it into a bowl and leave to cool to room temperature.

Put the remaining cream into a bowl and whisk until it starts to thicken. Whisk in the cooled icing sugar paste, a tablespoon at a time as quickly as you can, but don't overbeat. When the cream and sugar mixture are combined you should have a thick, glossy, spreadable icing. If the icing curdles, don't despair – it will still taste wonderful and it will set in the fridge.

If making the praline, line a baking tray with baking parchment. Put the caster sugar in an even layer in a saucepan. Leave it to melt over a medium-high heat, swirling every so often and moving the pan around so the sugar doesn't darken unevenly around the edges. When the sugar has liquified and turned golden brown, add the hazelnuts. Swirl them around in the caramel for a few moments, then turn out on to the baking tray.

Separate a few whole hazelnuts from the rest for decoration, then leave to cool completely. When the caramel is solid, break it up and blitz to crumbs in a food processor or blender or bash it with a rolling pin.

To assemble, take one of the cake rounds and brush it with more syrup. Grate over some of the chocolate until the base is completely covered, then spread over some of the icing. Grate over more chocolate, then put the second cake round on top. Brush with syrup then repeat with the chocolate, icing and more chocolate. Finally, place the third cake round on top.

Use the rest of the icing to cover the top and sides, then sprinkle with either the hazelnut praline crumbs and caramelised hazelnuts or more dark chocolate, grated or sliced into fine shards. Chill the cake in the fridge and remove it about 20 minutes before you want to serve it.

CARIBBEAN FRUIT CAKE

A beautiful alternative to a trad Christmas cake, this is based on the Caribbean black cake – so called because it contains blackened sugar to give it its dark colour. We just use ordinary brown sugar in our version, but it does have the lovely Caribbean flavours of rum and spices. The texture is moist and delicious and surprisingly light. Start soaking the fruit as far ahead as you can – at least six weeks but a few months is even better.

Makes at least 12 slices

Fruit

450g dried fruit – a mixture
    of raisins, sultanas and currants
100g prunes, roughly chopped
250ml golden rum or spiced rum
100ml Marsala
zest of 1 lime
1 tbsp treacle
1 tsp vanilla extract
1 tsp Angostura bitters
75g glacé cherries, rinsed and
    roughly chopped

Sponge

175g plain flour
1½ tsp baking powder
1 tsp mixed spice
1 tsp ground cinnamon
1 tsp ground allspice
rasp of nutmeg
pinch of salt
175g butter, softened
175g dark brown soft sugar
3 eggs

To finish

rum or brandy, for brushing
icing sugar for dusting

Put the dried fruit and prunes in a large container and cover them with the rum and Marsala. Seal and leave to soak for as long as possible – for weeks or even months. Shake or stir the fruit every so often.

When you are ready to make your cake, preheat your oven to 150°C/Fan 130°C/Gas 2. Grease a deep 22–23cm round cake tin and line it with baking parchment.

Put the fruit in a food processor with all the soaking liquor, the lime zest, treacle, vanilla extract and Angostura bitters. Pulse until you have a rough purée, then add the cherries.

Put the flour in a bowl with the baking powder, spices and a generous pinch of salt. Mix to combine.

Put the butter and brown sugar in a large bowl and beat until very soft and aerated. Add the eggs, one at a time with a tablespoon of the flour mixture, then fold in the remaining flour. Add the soaked fruit mixture and stir until it is completely combined.

Pour the mixture into the prepared tin and bake for about 2 hours until the cake has set and a skewer comes out clean. Remove from the oven. Brush the top with a little rum or brandy and leave it to cool in the tin. Brush the cake a couple more times as it cools – this will help prevent the top from drying out.

Wrap the cake in parchment and foil and store in an airtight tin until you are ready to eat it – it's best after it has had at least a few days to sit, but it can be eaten right away. Dust with icing sugar to serve.

MINT CHOC CHIP CAKE

From After Eights to choc chip ice cream, mint and chocolate have long been the best of friends and are ideal for a beautiful birthday cake. This is a great one for a kids' party – or anyone's party – and you can let your imagine run riot with the decoration.

Makes 8–12 slices

Sponge
200g plain flour
75g cocoa powder
225g sugar
1½ tsp baking powder
1 tsp bicarbonate of soda
pinch of salt
75g dark chocolate, finely
    chopped or coarsely grated
115g vegetable oil
1 tsp vanilla extract
3 eggs
175ml buttermilk
175ml just-boiled water

Mint choc chip buttercream

200g butter, softened
400g icing sugar
1–2 tbsp milk
up to 1 tsp peppermint extract
2–3 drops of green food
    colouring (optional)
75g dark chocolate, sliced
    into fine shards, plus extra
    to decorate

Preheat the oven to 180°C/Fan 160°C/Gas 4. Line 2 x 20–21cm sandwich tins with baking parchment.

Mix all the dry ingredients together with the dark chocolate. Put the vegetable oil in a separate bowl with the vanilla extract. Beat in the eggs, followed by the buttermilk, then gradually whisk in the just-boiled water.

Pour the wet ingredients into the dry and stir until just combined, keeping the mixing to an absolute minimum. Divide the mixture between the tins and bake for about 20 minutes until the cakes are well risen and springy to touch. Remove and turn the cakes out on to a cooling rack.

For the buttercream icing, beat the butter to loosen it, then gradually add the icing sugar, a couple of tablespoons at a time. Keep beating in between each addition until you have a thick, smooth icing. Add just enough milk to loosen the mixture to a very reluctant dropping consistency, then add the peppermint extract a few drops at a time, tasting as you go until you get the right strength. Make it slightly stronger than you think you need – it will taste very different when balanced by the chocolate.

Add the green food colouring, if using, a drop at a time until you have the colour you want. Then stir in the chocolate, keeping the stirring to a minimum.

When the cakes are cool, spread the top of one with a third of the icing. Place the second cake on top, then ice the top and sides with the remaining icing, making it as smooth as possible. This is much easier if you use a palette knife which you dip in freshly boiled water from time to time as you work. Decorate with more chocolate shards.

TEA
B

TIME
AKES

BLUE CHEESE & HAZELNUT SCONES

These are a very welcome addition to any tea table and you can make them bite-sized or larger – whatever takes your fancy. A crumbly blue cheese, such as Stilton is best, as it disperses through the mixture better than the creamier sort. And when you're eating these little beauties, don't be shy with the butter.

Makes 12–20

450g self-raising flour, plus extra
    for dusting
1 tsp baking powder
1 tsp salt
125g butter, chilled and diced
100g blue cheese, crumbled
    or diced
150ml whole milk
1 egg, beaten
2 tsp runny honey
40g hazelnuts, chopped
    or roughly crushed

For brushing

1 egg, beaten

Preheat the oven to 200°C/Fan 180°C/Gas 6. Line a baking tray with some baking parchment.

Put the flour, baking powder and salt in a food processor and add the butter. Mix until the texture resembles fine breadcrumbs, then add the blue cheese and mix again until it is evenly dispersed. You can, of course, do this by hand if you prefer.

Whisk the milk and egg together and add them to the mixture. Drizzle in the honey and add the hazelnuts. Mix as briefly as possible, just to combine, then turn out on to a floured surface.

Knead very briefly to bring everything together, then pat the dough out to a thickness of about 2.5cm. Dip a 4.5–5cm cutter in flour and cut out rounds – avoid twisting the cutter as you do so. Place the cut-out rounds on a baking tray. Use up any remaining dough in the same way – you should get about 20 scones in total – then brush with beaten egg. If you prefer larger scones, use a 6cm cutter and you will get about 12.

Bake the scones in the preheated oven for 10–12 minutes until well risen and lightly browned on top. Serve warm with butter, or leave them to cool, then store in an airtight container.

SAUSAGE PICNIC PIE

This is the perfect pie to take along for a picnic tea or to grace a high tea table. Pork and apple are always a happy combo and the apple mixture acts as a sort of instant chutney, adding a nice tang to contrast with the rich sausage meat.

Serves 4–6

Pastry

300g plain flour, plus extra
    for dusting
½ tsp baking powder
pinch of salt
75g butter, chilled and diced
75g suet or lard, chilled
1 egg, beaten
iced water

Filling

1 tbsp olive oil
1 onion, finely chopped
leaves from 1 thyme sprig
5 or 6 sage leaves, finely
    chopped
2 eating apples, peeled,
    cored and diced
50ml cider or apple juice
    or water
1 tbsp cider vinegar
1 tbsp demerara sugar
½ tsp ground allspice
1 tbsp wholegrain mustard
600g sausage meat
1 egg, beaten

First make the pastry. Put the flour and baking powder in a bowl and add a generous pinch of salt. Add the butter and the suet or lard and rub them into the flour until the mixture resembles fine breadcrumbs. Add the egg and just enough cold water to make a firm dough.

Dust your work surface with flour. Take three-quarters of the pastry and roll it out to fit a round, deep 16cm tin. Don't worry if the pastry breaks or cracks when you fit it in – simply press it well into the corners and make repairs with any trimmings. Add any unused trimmings to the pastry reserved for the lid. Chill the pastry in the fridge until you are ready to bake.

Heat the oil in a frying pan and add the onion. Fry over a low to medium heat until the onion is translucent but still has a little bite to it. Stir in the thyme, sage and apples and continue to cook for another 3 or 4 minutes. Add the cider, apple juice or water, together with the cider vinegar, sugar and allspice. Stir to combine and then bring the mixture to the boil. Simmer until most of the liquid has evaporated and the texture is verging on jammy.

Preheat the oven to 180°C/Fan 160°C/Gas 4.

To assemble, spread the mustard over the pastry base. Top with the sausage meat, pressing it down to compact it, then spread the apple mixture on top. Roll out the remaining pastry and use it to make a lid. Brush the edges with beaten egg and crimp them together. Brush the top of the pie with egg and cut a couple of vents in the centre to release steam.

Place the tin on a baking tray and bake for about 45 minutes until the crust is golden brown and the filling is piping hot. Good hot or cold.

CORNBREAD MUFFINS WITH BACON JAM

A touch of savoury bacon jam makes these muffins extra specially delicious. And they are naturally gluten-free if you go with all cornmeal, but you can also make them with half cornmeal, half flour if you want a softer crumb. They are at their best warm from the oven but once they've cooled, these are great spread with butter or some cream cheese.

Makes 12

300g fine cornmeal or
   150g cornmeal and
   150g plain flour
1 tbsp baking powder
1 tbsp caster sugar
pinch of salt
300ml buttermilk
2 eggs
60ml olive oil or melted butter
125g canned sweetcorn,
   drained and patted dry
2 tbsp pickled jalapeños,
   chopped (optional)
4 tbsp bacon jam (shop-bought
   or see p.259)

Preheat the oven to 200°C/Fan 180°C/Gas 6. Line a 12-hole muffin tin with paper cases.

Put the cornmeal or cornmeal and flour in a bowl with the baking powder, caster sugar and a generous pinch of salt. Stir to combine.

Put the buttermilk in a jug and beat in the eggs and the olive oil or melted butter. Pour this mixture into the bowl of dry ingredients and add the sweetcorn and the jalapeños, if using. Fold everything together, keeping the mixing to an absolute minimum. Don't worry if there's the odd streak of cornmeal – better to have that than an overmixed batter which makes for tough muffins.

Put a heaped tablespoon of the batter in each muffin case. Then top with a teaspoon of the bacon jam and give it a quick swirl to mix. Top with a further tablespoon of batter, followed by another half a teaspoon of bacon jam on top for a garnish. Push the bacon jam into the batter so it's flush with the batter rather than raised.

Bake the muffins in the oven for 15 minutes or until they are well risen and lightly browned. Enjoy warm or leave to cool.

SELKIRK BANNOCK

On our travels around the UK filming and feasting, we've both been fascinated by all the local varieties of bread and cakes to be found. The Selkirk bannock is one great example. A rich, fruity, yeasted concoction, it's said to have first been made by a baker in the town of Selkirk and served to Queen Victoria when she came to visit nearby Abbotsford House. A teatime treat fit for a queen!

Makes 1 loaf

175g raisins or sultanas
150ml whisky or strong tea
50g butter
50g lard (or another 50g butter)
275ml whole milk, plus extra for
  brushing
500g strong white flour
1 tsp mixed spice
½ tsp ground cinnamon
7g fast-acting yeast
50g light brown soft sugar
1 tsp salt
50g candied citrus peel,
  very finely chopped
  (optional)

Put the raisins or sultanas in a small saucepan and cover them with the whisky or strong tea. Bring to the boil, then remove the pan from the heat and leave to stand until completely cooled. Strain the raisins or sultanas and set aside.

Put the butter or the butter and lard in a small saucepan. Heat gently until melted, then add the milk. The milk should cool the fat to a tepid temperature just right for making the dough.

Put the flour, spices, yeast and sugar in a bowl and stir to combine, then add the salt. Add the drained raisins or sultanas and the citrus peel, if using. Gradually work in the butter and milk mixture until everything comes together into a dough. Knead for about 5 minutes until smooth and elastic – it will be quite a firm dough to work with.

Put the dough back in the bowl, cover with a damp cloth and leave to prove for 1–2 hours until doubled in size. Knock the dough back a little, then flatten it out into a rough oblong shape and roll it up as tightly as you can. Fold in the ends of the roll, then smooth and pull the dough into an oval or roundish free-form loaf. Place it on a baking tray lined with baking parchment and leave to prove again until the loaf is well risen and springy to touch.

Preheat the oven to 180°C/Fan 160°C/Gas 4. Bake the bannock for about 45 minutes until well risen and a rich brown. Brush it with a little milk, then put it back in the oven for a further 15–20 minutes.

Leave it on a wire rack until cool. Best served sliced, toasted and spread with salted butter.

GINGER & TREACLE SCONES

We love a nice scone and it's fun coming up with new variations. With these, dressed up with treacle, spices and stem ginger, we've hit the jackpot. You can make them in next to no time and they're good served with butter and some jam or lemon or lime curd.

Makes 12

450g self-raising flour,
   plus extra for dusting
1½ tsp baking powder
1 tsp ground ginger
½ tsp ground cinnamon
¼ tsp ground allspice
pinch of salt
125g butter
50g light brown soft sugar
2 tbsp treacle
3 balls of stem ginger,
   very finely chopped
150ml whole milk
1 egg, beaten

For brushing

1 tsp milk
1 tsp ginger syrup
   (from the jar)

Preheat the oven to 200°C/Fan 180°C/Gas 6 and line a baking tray with baking parchment.

Put the flour, baking powder and spices in a large bowl with a generous pinch of salt. Whisk briefly to remove any lumps.

Put the butter, sugar and treacle in a pan. Heat gently until melted together into a rich dark liquid, then stir in the chopped stem ginger. Remove from the heat and leave to cool for 5 minutes, then add the milk and egg.

Make a well in the flour and pour in the wet ingredients. Mix as briefly as possible to make a soft, still warm, dough, then turn it out on to a lightly floured surface.

Pat the dough into a round of about 3cm thick. Dip a 6cm cutter in flour and cut out rounds – avoid twisting the cutter as you do so. Place the rounds on the baking tray, then lightly knead the remaining offcuts and cut again. You should end up with 12 scones.

Mix the milk and syrup together and brush the mixture over the tops of the scones. Bake them in the preheated oven for 12–15 minutes until well risen. They will look quite craggy but will have a very light texture. Eat warm from the oven or leave to cool, then store in an airtight container.

SPICED TEACAKES

These are a lovely old-fashioned goody that we remember well from our childhoods. What you want from a teacake is a good amount of surface for slathering with lots of butter, so we like to make ours quite flat and wide – that way they are easier to drop into the toaster too. You can use this same recipe for making hot cross buns (see below).

Makes 12

50g butter, melted
1 egg, well beaten
500g strong white flour,
    plus extra for dusting
7g fast-acting yeast
50g golden caster sugar
1 tsp mixed spice
1½ tsp salt
200g raisins or sultanas
50g candied citrus peel, very
    finely chopped (optional)
zest of 1 orange

Infused milk

300ml milk
5 cardamom pods
6 cloves
3cm piece of cinnamon stick
½ tsp allspice berries

Start by infusing the milk. Put the milk in a small pan, then lightly crush the spices and add them to the pan. Bring the milk to just under boiling point, then remove the pan from the heat and leave the milk to infuse.

When the milk has cooled to room temperature, strain and discard the spices. Pour the melted butter into the milk, then add all but a tablespoon of the egg to the milk and beat together. Set the reserved egg aside for later.

Put the flour in a large bowl and add the yeast, sugar and mixed spice. Give it a quick stir to disperse the yeast, then add the salt. Add the raisins or sultanas, the candied peel, if using, and the orange zest.

Gradually work in the infused milk mixture until you have a sticky dough. Cover the bowl with a damp tea towel and leave the dough to stand for half an hour to give the gluten a chance to start working. Turn the dough out on to a floured surface and knead until smooth and no longer sticky.

Put the dough back in the bowl and cover with a damp tea towel again, then leave to prove until it has doubled in size.

Knock the dough back and divide it into 12 pieces. Knead each piece of dough into a ball, trying to make sure that all the raisins are covered with a 'skin' of dough to prevent them from burning in the oven. Then roll each ball until fairly flat with a diameter of 9–10cm. Arrange the balls on a couple of baking trays, spacing them out well, and cover them with a damp tea towel. Leave to rise.

Preheat the oven to 200°C/Fan 180°C/Gas 6. Mix the reserved tablespoon of egg with a little water. When the teacakes have doubled in size again, brush them carefully with the beaten egg, then bake for 20–25 minutes. They should rise to a dome shape in the oven and turn a rich golden brown. Enjoy them warm or leave to cool, then split and toast.

HOT CROSS BUNS
To make this mixture into hot cross buns, don't flatten the balls of dough out quite so much and arrange them on one baking tray – they will spread towards one another during proving and baking. To make the cross, mix 50ml of water with 50ml of flour to make a thick paste. Pipe or spoon crosses over the buns. Bake as above.

BANANAS FOSTER BLONDIES

Bananas Foster is a famous dish in New Orleans and consists of bananas caramelised in lots of butter, sugar and rum, then served with ice cream. We cooked it there once and inspired by this wonderful dessert, we came up with the idea of using the bananas to top a blondie tray bake, flavoured with coconut and pecans. What more can we say? This is fabulous – a proper Hairy Bikers' mash-up.

Makes 16 squares

50g desiccated coconut
200g plain flour
½ tsp baking powder
50g pecans, roughly chopped
175g butter, melted and cooled
225g light brown soft sugar
pinch of salt
2 eggs
1 tsp vanilla extract

Caramelised bananas

2 small, fairly firm bananas
25g butter
50g light brown soft sugar
¼ tsp ground cinnamon
zest of ½ lime
2 tbsp dark rum

Preheat the oven to 200°C/Fan 180°C/Gas 6. Line a 20cm square tin with baking parchment.

Put the coconut in a dry frying pan and toast it over a medium heat, stirring regularly, until it is lightly golden all over. Remove from the heat and leave to cool. Mix the cooled coconut in a bowl with the flour, baking powder and chopped pecans.

Put the melted butter in a separate bowl and add the sugar and a pinch of salt. Beat until completely combined – and there isn't a slick of butter on top – then beat in the eggs and vanilla extract. Fold in the dry ingredients and scrape the batter into the prepared tin.

Slice the bananas on the diagonal, aiming to get 8 pieces from each banana. Put the butter and sugar in a frying pan and heat gently, stirring regularly until the sugar has dissolved and the mixture is no longer gritty. Add the cinnamon, lime zest and rum and continue to stir until the sauce is a deep golden brown.

Add the slices of banana and turn up the heat slightly. Cook the bananas for a couple of minutes on each side – keep a careful eye on them, as you don't want them to get remotely mushy – then remove them from the heat. Leave to cool for few minutes.

Arrange the bananas over the batter, then drizzle over any of the remaining caramel. Bake in the preheated oven for about 25 minutes, until the cake is light brown with a shiny top.

Remove from the oven. Leave to cool to room temperature, then cut into 16 squares. Store in an airtight tin.

BROWN BUTTER CUPCAKES

Using brown sugar and brown butter gives these cupcakes a beautiful, slightly biscuity flavour, which we love. Instead of buttercream, we used ermine icing which is a little less sweet. It's also easy to make into swirls, so you can have lots of fun getting creative. We enjoyed making these look like little soft-scoop ice creams.

Makes 12

175g plain flour
1 tsp baking powder
¼ tsp bicarbonate of soda
pinch of salt
125g brown butter, softened
   (see p.275)
50g light brown soft sugar
25g dark brown soft sugar
   (or another 25g light brown
   soft sugar)
50ml maple syrup
2 eggs
75ml buttermilk
a few drops of vanilla extract
1 tbsp demerara sugar
   (optional)

Strawberry sauce

300g strawberries
squeeze of lemon juice
25g icing sugar
pinch of salt

Ermine icing

40g flour
225ml whole milk
125g caster sugar
pinch of salt
225g butter, softened
½ tsp vanilla extract

To serve

hundreds and thousands
   or similar
4 chocolate flakes, cut into thirds

Preheat the oven to 180°C/Fan 160°C/Gas 4 and line a cupcake tin with 12 paper cases.

Put the flour in a bowl with the baking powder, bicarbonate of soda and a generous pinch of salt. Whisk to remove any lumps.

Put the brown butter in a bowl with the brown sugars and maple syrup. Beat with electric beaters until very soft and well aerated. Add an egg and 2 tablespoons of the flour mixture, then beat until well combined. Add another egg and 2 tablespoons of the flour and mix again. Add the remaining flour, then fold in the buttermilk and vanilla extract.

Spoon the mixture into the cupcake cases – each one should take a heaped tablespoon. Sprinkle over a little demerara sugar, if using, for extra crunch. Bake the cakes in the preheated oven for 20–25 minutes until well risen and golden brown. Leave to cool.

To make the strawberry sauce, purée the strawberries with the lemon juice, sugar and a pinch of salt. Push everything through a sieve if you want to remove the tiny seeds, then chill until needed – the mixture will thicken.

To make the icing, put the flour in a saucepan. Place over a medium heat and gradually whisk in the milk. When it is all incorporated, stir or whisk until the mixture thickens to a paste the texture of a thick béchamel. It will do so quite suddenly, so make sure you stir constantly. Remove from the heat and transfer the mixture to a bowl. Beat in the sugar with a generous pinch of salt until the sugar dissolves and the sauce thins out a little. It may have an unappetising grey tinge to it at this point, but don't worry, it will not affect the finished icing. Cover and leave to cool to room temperature. You can also chill the paste at this point until you are ready to use it.

Put the butter in a bowl and beat with electric beaters until it's very soft and aerated. Give the flour and milk paste a good whisk, just to make sure it is lump-free, then gradually add it to the butter, a tablespoon at a time until it is all incorporated. Add the vanilla extract and beat again for 2 or 3 minutes, then taste. Add a little more vanilla extract if necessary and beat again. You can store this icing in the fridge for several days before using it if you like.

To assemble, pipe the icing over the cupcakes in a swirl to resemble soft-scoop ice cream, then sprinkle over some hundreds and thousands or similar. Add a flake and serve with the strawberry sauce.

BLUEBERRY SKYR MUFFINS

Skyr is an Icelandic version of yoghurt but is thicker and creamier in texture and is very delicious. It works really well with the honey and vanilla in these blueberry muffins, which we first made when filming at a skyr farm in the Peak District. The crew hoovered these up as soon as they were out of the oven and that's always a good sign!

Makes 12

240g plain flour
1 tsp baking powder
½ tsp bicarbonate of soda
100g caster sugar
pinch of salt
100ml butter, melted
150ml skyr
2 eggs, beaten
1 tsp vanilla extract
2 tbsp milk
50ml runny honey
150g blueberries
granulated or demerara sugar,
   for sprinkling

Preheat the oven to 200°C/Fan 180°C/Gas 6 and line a deep, 12-hole muffin tin with paper cases.

Mix the flour, baking powder, bicarb and sugar in a large bowl and add a generous pinch of salt.

Mix the butter, skyr, eggs, vanilla extract, milk and honey together in a jug, then add the mixture to the flour along with the blueberries. Mix to combine, keeping the stirring to a minimum – this helps keep the muffins tender.

Spoon the mixture into the muffin cases – they will be very full, but this is fine. Sprinkle granulated or demerara sugar over the tops and bake the muffins in the preheated oven for about 20 minutes until they are well risen and deeply coloured. Leave to cool or enjoy them warm from the oven.

DATE SLICES

These are a good old-fashioned treat that shouldn't be forgotten. You might be a little surprised at the addition of coffee, but trust us – you don't notice it but it works with the vanilla to provide a bit of extra oomph. These are mega tasty and with the wholemeal flour, oats and dates, they're packed with healthy fibre, so are quite good for you too. Don't be tempted to leave out the salt – it really boosts the flavour.

Makes 8 slices

Base and topping
125g wholemeal flour
100g plain flour
½ tsp baking powder
pinch of salt
150g butter, chilled and diced
100g porridge oats
75g light brown soft sugar
1 egg yolk

Filling
350g pitted dates, chopped
50ml freshly brewed coffee
½ tsp vanilla extract
¼ tsp cinnamon
pinch of salt

Preheat the oven to 170°C/Fan 150°C/Gas 3½. Line a 20–21cm square baking tin with baking parchment.

Put the flours and baking powder in a bowl with a good pinch of salt. Add the butter and rub it in until the mixture resembles breadcrumbs, then stir in the oats and sugar. Divide the mixture in half. Mix the egg yolk into one half of the mixture and press it into the lined tin. Set the rest of the mixture aside.

Put the dates in a saucepan with the coffee, vanilla, cinnamon, a generous pinch of salt and 100ml of water. Heat, stirring regularly and breaking up the dates with the edge of a spoon, until you have a thick paste. Remove the pan from the heat and leave to cool.

Spread the cooled date mixture over the base in the tin. Take the remaining flour mixture and squeeze handfuls of it together, then break these up to form clumps. Sprinkle the clumps over the dates as evenly as possible and press them down lightly.

Bake in the oven for 25–30 minutes until golden brown, then leave to cool in the tin. Remove from the tin and cut into 8 slices.

GROUND RICE TARTS

We both remember our mams and aunties making tarts and cakes with ground rice, an old-fashioned and cheaper alternative to ground almonds. It's an idea well worth resurrecting, we think, so do give these a try. Raspberry jam is traditional in this sort of bake, but feel free to use your favourite flavour.

Makes 12

Pastry
200g plain flour, plus extra
   for dusting
pinch of salt
100g butter, chilled and diced
1 tbsp icing sugar
1 egg yolk
iced water

Sponge

110g ground rice
15g plain flour
pinch of salt
125g butter, softened
125g caster sugar
1 egg, beaten

To assemble

raspberry jam

First make the pastry. Put the flour in a bowl with a pinch of salt and add the butter. Rub it into the flour until the mixture resembles fine breadcrumbs, then stir in the icing sugar. Whisk the egg yolk with a tablespoon of iced water and mix it in, then add just enough iced water to bind everything together into a dough. Knead very lightly until smooth.

Turn the pastry out on to a floured work surface and roll it out thinly. Cut out 12 x 10cm rounds and use them to line a 12-hole muffin tin – the pastry edges should be flush with the top of the tin. Chill for at least an hour.

Preheat the oven to 180°C/Fan 160°C/Gas 4.

To make the sponge, mix the ground rice and flour together with a pinch of salt. Put the butter and sugar in a separate bowl and beat until well combined and fluffy, then add the egg and the rice and flour mixture. Fold everything together until you have a fairly stiff batter.

Put half a teaspoon of jam in the base of each pastry case, then top with a heaped tablespoon of the sponge batter. Bake for about 20 minutes until the pastry is golden and the sponge has puffed up and is lightly browned. They should have a slightly domed appearance and a light, crisp top.

Leave the tarts to cool in the tin, then remove and store in an airtight container.

BAKLAVA

A lavish confection of filo, honey and nuts, baklava is a traditional treat in Turkey, Greece and other eastern European countries and is not as hard to make as you might think. It's traditionally made with pistachios but works well with walnuts – which are much cheaper!

Makes about 40 pieces

Filling
500g walnuts
1 tsp ground cinnamon
zest of 1 orange
pinch of salt
50g butter, melted

Pastry
24 sheets of filo
200ml butter, melted

Syrup
250g granulated sugar
100g runny honey
a few pieces of pared
   orange zest

Orange and cardamom cream
(optional)
400ml whipping or double
   cream
½ tsp orange zest, very finely
   chopped
1 tbsp icing sugar
½ tsp ground cardamom

Grind 150g of the walnuts quite finely but not to a powder – aim for a texture similar to ground almonds. Chop the remaining walnuts and mix them with the ground walnuts. Add the cinnamon and orange zest and a generous pinch of salt, then stir in the melted butter. Set aside.

Take a large, straight-sided baking tin measuring about 30 x 25cm. Line it with 2 pieces of foil, which cross one another and overhang each side. This will help you remove the baklava from the tin later. Preheat the oven to 160°C/Fan 140°C/Gas 3.

Brush the foil with butter. Take the filo sheets and trim them to fit the tin – you will probably need 2 sheets to cover the base of the tin. Lay the filo over the buttered foil and brush with more butter. Repeat until you have 6 layers of filo.

Sprinkle over the nut mixture as evenly as you can, but make sure you don't press it down too much – you don't want it compressed. Then top with more filo and butter and keep going until you have another 6 layers of filo on top.

Next, slice the baklava as shown opposite, cutting through to the filling in parallel lines. Bake in the oven for about 35 minutes until the top layer of pastry is a rich golden brown.

Meanwhile, make the syrup. Put the sugar and honey in a saucepan with 150ml of water and the orange zest. Heat gently until the sugar and honey have melted, then simmer for about 10 minutes until the consistency is syrupy.

When you have removed the baklava from the oven, leave it to cool. Reheat the syrup if necessary and pour it evenly over the pastry. Leave to cool for at least an hour, preferably for a few hours.

Remove the baklava from the tin and cut back through the lines, this time right through to the base – a metal dough scraper is really good for this, as is a long knife, as you can just press it down instead of pulling it through. Store in an airtight container. Serve with the orange and cardamom cream, if you like.

For the orange and cardamom cream, if using, put the whipping or double cream in a large bowl with the orange zest. Whisk by hand or with electric beaters until the cream is soft and billowy. Mix the icing sugar with the cardamom and stir it into the cream.

BISCOFF BROWNIES

These are extra-special brownies made with those much-loved Biscoff biscuits and spread. We're serious about our method for layering up the ingredients for melting. If you simply chuck everything in, the sugar doesn't dissolve properly and you don't get the right texture. Yes, we're bossy but you love us!

Makes 9 squares

75g plain flour
½ tsp baking powder
pinch of salt
150g butter, diced
250g caster sugar
75g dark chocolate, broken up
85g cocoa powder
2 eggs
1 tsp vanilla extract

Additions

9 or 10 Biscoff biscuits
150g Biscoff spread (smooth
 or crunchy)

Preheat the oven to 160°C/Fan 140°C/Gas 3. Line a 20 x 20cm square brownie tin with baking parchment.

Mix the flour and baking powder together with a generous pinch of salt.

Put the butter in a heatproof bowl. Pour the sugar over it, then add the dark chocolate and finally the cocoa powder. It's important to layer the ingredients up in this order, as this will help them melt together evenly. Set the bowl over a saucepan of gently simmering water and leave, stirring very occasionally, until the butter and chocolate has melted and most of the sugar has dissolved. It will take a while. The mixture will be quite liquid until you stir it, then it will thicken. Don't worry if it is a bit grainy at this stage. Leave it to cool for 5 minutes.

Now beat in the eggs, one at a time, making sure they are completely amalgamated. If the mixture starts to look oily and come away from the side of the bowl in a large block, just whisk vigorously with a balloon whisk until it becomes stickier again. Stir in the vanilla extract.

Add the flour mixture and beat it in until no white streaks remain. Continue beating for another minute until you have a smooth, glossy batter that's just about pourable.

Arrange the biscuits over the base of the brownie tin – be as regimented or as random as you like. Pour over the brownie batter, making sure the biscuits are completely covered, then smooth over the top as evenly as possible with a palette knife.

Drop teaspoons of Biscoff spread over the top of the batter. Use a palette knife to push the dollops of spread down until they are flush with the batter. Make a few swirls with the palette knife or a cocktail stick.

Bake the brownies in the preheated oven for 20–25 minutes until they have a crisp coating and a skewer comes out with crumbs sticking to it. Leave to cool completely in the tin before cutting it into squares.

If you can bear to wait, put the brownies in the fridge overnight as this will really improve their texture. Then transfer them to an airtight tin.

PEAR TARTLETS

These are real proper fancy French patisserie – like you see in shop windows in France. They're very impressive and much of the prep can be done in advance, as the tartlets are served chilled. If you don't want to poach pears, you could use tinned pears or any berries or soft fruit uncooked – just add the fruit to the tarts and glaze as described.

Makes 6

Almond pastry
75g plain flour, plus extra
    for dusting
75g ground almonds
pinch of salt
75g butter, chilled
2 tsp icing sugar
1 egg yolk
iced water

Pears

4 small pears, peeled, halved
    and cored
juice and pared zest of ½ lemon
100ml white wine
200g caster sugar
1 tbsp pear eau de vie (optional)

Crème patissière

200ml whole milk
1 vanilla pod, split lengthways
a few drops of almond extract
50g golden caster sugar
15g cornflour
pinch of salt
2 egg yolks
10g butter, chilled and diced

To glaze

1 tbsp jam (apricot, pear, apple)
1 tsp pear eau de vie (optional)

To make the pastry, put the flour and ground almonds in a bowl with a pinch of salt and mix gently. Add the butter and rub it into the flour until the mixture resembles fine breadcrumbs, then stir in the icing sugar. Mix the egg yolk with a little iced water, then work this into the mix – add a little more water if necessary to bind the dough together.

Knead the dough gently until smooth. Lightly dust your work surface with flour and roll the pastry out as thinly as you can. Using a 12cm cutter, cut out rounds to line 6 tartlet tins. Chill them in the fridge for at least 30 minutes.

Preheat the oven to 180°C/Fan 160°C/Gas 4. Put the tartlet tins on a baking tray. Line them with baking parchment and fill with baking beans. Bake for 15 minutes, then remove the beans and parchment and put the tartlet tins back in the oven for another 8–10 minutes until the pastry is completely cooked. Remove them from the oven and leave to cool.

To poach the pears, first cut out a round of baking parchment to fit the saucepan you are going to use. Toss the pears in lemon juice. Put the lemon zest in the pan with the wine, sugar and 650ml of water. Heat slowly, stirring to dissolve the sugar, then add the pears to the pan. Scrunch and unscrunch the baking parchment and lay it on top of the pears – this will stop them rising above the liquid line. Leave the pears to simmer gently for about an hour, until they are knife tender all the way through. Add the eau de vie, if using, and leave the pears to cool in the poaching liquid.

To make the crème patissière, put the milk in a pan with the vanilla pod and bring it to just below boiling point. Remove the pan from the heat and leave the milk to infuse for half an hour. Whisk the sugar and cornflour together with a pinch of salt, then add the egg yolks. Whisk until pale yellow and foamy – the mixture will look very thick and dry to start with but will soon loosen up. Pour the milk over the egg mixture from a height, discarding the vanilla pod. Whisk constantly as you do so, then pour everything back into the pan.

Cook the mixture over a low heat until it starts to thicken. Continue to cook, whisking constantly and thoroughly, as the mixture can easily become lumpy at this stage. When it starts to bubble, continue to cook for another minute, then remove from the heat. Beat in the butter until you have a thick, smooth, glossy custard, then pour this through a sieve into a bowl or container. Cover with cling film, making sure it touches the surface of the custard to prevent a skin from forming, then leave to cool to room temperature. Transfer the bowl to the fridge and leave to chill for at least a couple of hours.

Spoon the crème patissière into the pastry cases. Remove the pears from the poaching liquor, drain them thoroughly, then pat with kitchen paper until they are as dry as possible. Slice each half thinly, but keep the slices attached at the top. Arrange the slices in a fan over the crème patissière in each tartlet. Slice any halves left over to fill any gaps.

Heat the jam, adding the eau de vie, if using, and brush it over the pears. Chill until ready to serve.

PEANUT BUTTER & JAM TARTS

Peanut butter and jam – or jelly as Americans say – are a classic combo and gave us the genius idea of making good old jam tarts a bit special. These are really easy to make, but you do need to make sure you spread the first layer of peanut butter as evenly as you can so it doesn't clump. We find that crunchy seems to spread more easily than smooth.

Makes 12

Pastry
175g plain flour, plus extra
    for dusting
90g butter, chilled and diced
pinch of salt
2 tsp icing sugar
1 egg yolk
iced water

Filling

6 heaped tsp peanut butter,
    crunchy or smooth
300g soft-set jam

First make the pastry. Put the flour in a bowl with the butter and a good pinch of salt. Rub the butter into the flour until it resembles fine breadcrumbs, then stir in the icing sugar and egg yolk. Add just enough iced water to bind the mixture into a smooth dough, making sure it isn't too crumbly.

Lightly dust your work surface with flour and roll out the pastry. Cut 12 x 7.5cm rounds and use these to line a 12-hole fairy cake tin. Chill the pastry in the fridge for half an hour.

Preheat the oven to 180°C/Fan 160°C/Gas 4. Put a scant half teaspoon of peanut butter in the centre of each pastry round and spread it out so it coats the base evenly. Give the jam a good stir to make sure it is soft and not too set. Put a generously heaped teaspoon (about 25g) of jam over the peanut butter in each tart, sealing round the edges to make sure the peanut butter is completely covered.

Bake for 15–18 minutes until the pastry is golden and the jam has bubbled up. Remove from the oven and leave to cool before eating – the jam will be blisteringly hot!

BISC

COC

CHEESE SHORTBREAD

Shortbread doesn't have to come in a tartan tin! You might think that making 40 of these is a bit over the top on our part, but be warned – no one can eat just one. And once you start, you can't stop. The dough freezes well, though, so if you like, pop one of the logs in the freezer for another time. You can slice and bake the dough from frozen or defrost it first, as you prefer. Really hard cheeses, such as Parmesan, mature Cheddar or Gruyère, work best and be sure to grate the cheese as finely as possible.

Makes 40

150g plain flour, plus extra
   for dusting
100g butter, chilled and diced
pinch of salt
85g Cheddar, Parmesan,
   Gruyère or similar, finely
   grated

Optional extras
1 tsp dried thyme or rosemary
½ tsp cayenne or chipotle
   powder
1 tsp caraway or cumin seeds

Put the flour, butter and a generous pinch of salt in a food processor and process until completely combined – the mixture should go just beyond the fine breadcrumbs stage and start clumping together. Add the cheese and process again until the mixture forms into a dough. You can do all this by hand if you prefer, of course.

Turn the dough out on to a lightly floured work surface and knead very briefly until smooth. Divide it in half and roll each piece into a log of about 4cm in diameter. Wrap and chill in the fridge for an hour.

When you are ready to bake the biscuits, preheat the oven to 180°C/Fan 160°C/Gas 4. Line 2 baking trays with baking parchment. Cut the logs into rounds – each should be about 5mm thick – and arrange them on the baking trays. You should have about 40 biscuits. Sprinkle with any of the optional extras that take your fancy.

Bake the shortbread in the preheated oven for 15–18 minutes until very lightly brown around the edges. Remove from the oven and leave to cool on the trays. Store in an airtight container.

CLASSIC OATMEAL COOKIES

Made with wholemeal flour and porridge oats, these cookies are healthy and a good satisfying eat. And if you like, you can swap out the dried apple for raisins, or even chocolate chips. If you do use choc chips, we recommend leaving out the spices.

Makes 24

150g wholemeal plain flour
1 tsp bicarbonate of soda
1 tsp ground cinnamon
¼ tsp ground cloves
pinch of salt
100g butter, softened
150g light brown soft sugar
25g granulated sugar
1 egg
100g porridge oats
100g dried apple, finely
  chopped

Preheat the oven to 170°C/Fan 150°C/Gas 3½. Line 2 large baking trays with baking parchment – you'll need to bake the cookies in 2 batches.

Put the flour, bicarb, cinnamon and cloves in a bowl with a generous pinch of salt and whisk together.

In a separate bowl, beat the butter and sugars together until very soft and aerated. Beat in the egg, followed by the flour mixture, oats and dried apple.

Spoon scant tablespoons of the mixture on to the baking trays and shape them into rounds. Make sure you space them well apart – you should be able to get 6 on to each tray.

Bake the cookies for 12–15 minutes until they have spread and flattened out and have taken on a light golden-brown colour. They will still be soft and a little puffy, but they will firm up and sink once they've cooled down.

As soon as the cookies have set enough for you to be able to move them, transfer them to a rack to cool. Then spoon out the remaining mixture on to the baking trays and bake as above.

These are quite chewy cookies, but for a crunchier result, leave them in the oven for a few more minutes. They will firm up even more when cool and they'll have more of a snap. Once cool, store in an airtight container.

GINGERNUTS

A total classic, the gingernut has everything you want from a biscuit and it's really worth trying our home-made version. It's crisp, full of flavour and great for dunking in your tea. We like to add a little chopped stem ginger for extra chew.

Makes about 24

225g self-raising flour
2 tbsp ground ginger
½ tsp bicarbonate of soda
150g light brown soft sugar
pinch of salt
75g golden syrup
75g butter
1 egg yolk
3 pieces of stem ginger,
   finely chopped

Preheat the oven to 180°C/Fan 160°C/Gas 4. Line 2 baking trays with baking parchment.

Put the flour, ginger, bicarbonate of soda and sugar in a large bowl and add a generous pinch of salt.

Put the golden syrup and butter in a pan and melt them together over a gentle heat. Make a well in the flour and pour in the melted syrup and butter, then add the egg yolk and stem ginger.

Mix thoroughly into a dough. The dough might seem quite crumbly at first, but don't worry, it will clump together eventually.

Working with damp hands, pinch off pieces of dough the size of large walnuts (they should weigh about 25g each) and place them on the baking trays. They will spread and flatten, so space them out well. Press them down slightly – they may crack a little around the edges. You should end up with about 24.

Bake the biscuits in the preheated oven for 12–15 minutes until they are golden-brown with a cracked surface. They will still be soft and slightly puffed up. Leave them to cool and firm up on the baking trays, then store in an airtight tin.

BILLIONAIRE'S SHORTBREAD

Who wants to be a millionaire when you can be a billionaire? This is what you make when Elon Musk comes to tea! Not for the faint-hearted – or the dieter – but gob-smackingly good. If you really want to go for the bling, sprinkle on some gold leaf.

Makes 16 squares

Shortbread base
150g butter, softened
75g caster sugar
pinch of salt
175g plain flour
50g medium cornmeal
   or rice flour

Caramel filling

175g butter
175g light brown soft sugar
75g golden syrup
1 x 397g can of condensed milk
½–1 tsp sea salt, to taste

Topping

50g butter, diced
150g dark chocolate (or 50/50
   dark and milk if you prefer)
½ tsp sea salt flakes

Preheat the oven to 180°C/Fan 160°C/Gas 4. Line a 20–21cm square tin with baking parchment, leaving enough overhang so can you can lift the shortbread out when it's made.

For the shortbread base, put the butter and sugar in a bowl with a generous pinch of salt and beat together lightly to form a grainy paste. Add the flour and the cornmeal or rice flour and mix together – it will initially form clumps. Use your hands to bring everything together into a dough, then press it into the tin, as evenly as possible. Prick the dough all over with a fork, then bake it in the preheated oven for 25–30 minutes until it is golden around the edges. Remove from the oven and leave to cool.

Meanwhile, prepare the caramel filling. Put all the ingredients into a saucepan then heat together gently, stirring until everything has melted into a sauce. Turn up the heat a little to somewhere between a simmer and a boil and keep stirring regularly so the sauce doesn't catch around the edges – watch it carefully as it may splutter a little. Continue cooking for 20–25 minutes while the sauce gradually thickens and darkens.

To check the caramel is ready, remove the pan from the heat and leave the sauce to cool for a few minutes. If you press it with your finger, your finger should come away completely clear and the indentation should slowly disappear. Once the caramel is ready, pour it over the shortbread. When it has cooled to room temperature, transfer the tin to the fridge so the caramel can chill and harden.

To make the topping, put the butter and chocolate in a heatproof bowl and place the bowl over a pan of simmering water. When both have melted, whisk them into a smooth, runny sauce and pour this over the caramel. Give the tin a very gentle shake – this will encourage the chocolate to smooth out, so it's completely even. If there are any air bubbles, pick the tin up and drop it gently on to your work surface a couple of times to get rid of them. Sprinkle the top with the salt and put the tin back in the fridge for the topping to set.

When the chocolate has set completely, remove the tin from the fridge. Using the parchment, lift the shortbread out of the tin. Lightly oil a knife or a straight-bladed metal kitchen scraper and carefully cut the shortbread into squares. Store in an airtight tin.

CARAMELISED ALMOND & RAISIN COOKIES

There are a lot of great cookies out there nowadays and we want to introduce you to our latest beauty. These are really tasty cookies, given extra crunch by the caramelised almonds. Good for a teatime snack or to pack into a lunch box for a post-sandwich treat.

Makes 24 cookies

175g plain flour
¼ tsp bicarbonate of soda
¼ tsp baking powder
pinch of salt
125g butter, softened
100g light brown soft sugar
100g granulated sugar
125g almond butter
1 egg
½ tsp vanilla extract
100g raisins

Caramelised almonds

50g granulated sugar
100g almonds (skin on is fine)

First caramelise the almonds. Put the sugar in a frying pan with 75ml of water. Slowly bring to the boil, stirring until the sugar has dissolved, then keep stirring as the liquid thickens to a syrup.

Add the almonds and continue to cook, while stirring constantly, until the syrup darkens, becomes sticky and eventually turns to a powder around the almonds. This does take a little while, so be patient. Remove the frying pan from the heat, then tip the almonds on to a plate lined with greaseproof paper to cool. Roughly chop half the almonds, then finely chop the rest to the consistency of coarse breadcrumbs.

Preheat the oven to 170°C/Fan 150°C/Gas 3½. Line 3 baking trays with baking parchment.

Put the flour, bicarb and baking powder in a bowl with a pinch of salt and mix thoroughly. Put the butter and sugars in a separate bowl and beat until well combined and aerated. Beat in the almond butter, followed by the egg and the vanilla extract. Add all the dry ingredients and the raisins to the butter mixture and mix to form a soft, thick dough.

Scoop spoonfuls of the mixture and space them out over the baking trays – each cookie should be roughly a heaped tablespoon – and flatten them down lightly. If you want to be really accurate, weigh the mixture first and divide it by 24 to get an idea of how big each cookie should be.

Bake the cookies for 12–14 minutes until well spread out and golden brown around the edges – this will give you a chewy-centred cookie. For a crunchier cookie, leave for a couple of minutes longer.

Remove the cookies from the oven and leave them to cool on the baking trays. Store in an airtight container.

CHOCOLATE CHILLI COOKIES

We first made a version of these at Big Jim's chilli farm in New Mexico and we thought they'd be a great souvenir to bring home and share with you all. You can make these lush little numbers with ordinary dark chocolate if you like, but if you're a fan of a bit of heat, go for the chilli version and give yourself a treat. These will wake up your taste buds.

Makes 24

150g plain flour
50g cocoa powder
1 tsp bicarbonate of soda
½ tsp ground cinnamon
½ tsp cayenne (or to taste)
pinch of salt
125g butter, softened
50g golden caster sugar
150g dark brown soft sugar
1 egg
2 tsp vanilla extract
100g dark chilli chocolate,
    roughly chopped

Preheat the oven to 170°C/Fan 150°C/Gas 3½.

Put the flour in a bowl with the cocoa powder, bicarbonate of soda, spices and a generous pinch of salt. Mix together thoroughly.

In a separate bowl, beat the butter with the sugars with an electric hand whisk until very soft and aerated. Beat in the egg and vanilla extract, then fold in the dry ingredients and the chocolate.

Divide the mixture into 24 balls. Place them on a couple of baking trays, spacing them out well so they don't run into one another.

Bake the cookies in the preheated oven for about 12 minutes until they have spread and have a cracked appearance. They may puff up, but this will subside when they have cooled a little.

Remove the cookies from the oven and leave them on the trays for a minute or so to firm up, then transfer them to a cooling rack. The cookies should be fairly flat, cracked and have chewy centres. Store them in an airtight tin.

CHERRY VIENNESE WHIRLS

Said to have been inspired by an Austrian filled biscuit, Viennese whirls are pretty little piped biscuits, filled with buttercream and jam. They're always delicious but even better when you bake your own and you can make them any shape you like. Play some Johann Strauss and indulge – teatime doesn't get better than this.

Makes about 16 sandwich biscuits

Biscuits
250g butter, softened
50g icing sugar
250g plain flour
50g cornflour
½ tsp vanilla extract
pinch of salt

Filling
100g butter, softened
200g icing sugar, sieved
a few drops of vanilla extract
   or kirsch
up to 2 tbsp milk
50g dark chocolate, grated
   (optional)
75g cherry jam or conserve

To serve
icing sugar, for dusting

Line 2 baking trays with baking parchment. Put all the biscuit ingredients into a bowl and beat together to make a smooth, soft paste. Chill the dough in the fridge for 15 minutes.

Fit a star nozzle in a piping bag. Spoon in half the mixture, then pipe it out on to the baking tray, spacing the biscuits well apart. The shape is up to you – you can do small swirls, stars or strips. Then repeat with the remaining batter and you should end up with about 32 biscuits.

Chill the piped biscuits for at least half an hour, longer if it is a very hot day. This will help them keep their shape. When you are ready to bake the biscuits, preheat the oven to 190°C/Fan 170°C/Gas 5.

Bake the biscuits for 13–15 minutes until they are a pale golden colour and cooked through. Leave them to cool on the tray.

To make the filling, put the butter and icing sugar in a bowl and mix together. Use a spoon to start with, as this gives you more control and stops the icing sugar from flying everywhere. Once the mixture is crumbly, use electric beaters or beat more vigorously with a spoon until the mixture is very soft and light – it will increase a lot in volume too. Stir through the vanilla or kirsch and just enough milk to loosen the mixture a bit.

Using a palette knife, spread some of the filling on the underside of half the biscuits. Sprinkle with grated chocolate, if using. Spread the underside of the remaining biscuits with the jam or conserve, then sandwich together.

Leave the biscuits to set – chill them for half an hour if necessary – then store in an airtight tin. Dust with icing sugar before serving.

SICILIAN FIG ROLLS

We've all enjoyed a few fig rolls at some point in our life, but these are a bit special. Adding a touch of Marsala and citrus zest gives this old favourite a touch of Sicilian glamour. These are the best – the godfather of all biscuits!

Makes 32

Pastry
275g plain flour
75g ground almonds
1 tsp baking powder
pinch of salt
175g butter, chilled and diced
1 egg, beaten
milk

Filling
75g raisins, roughly chopped
125ml Marsala
350g soft, ready-to-eat dried figs, trimmed
75g almonds or pine nuts, very finely chopped
zest of 1 lemon
zest of ½ orange
½ tsp ground cinnamon
1 tbsp honey
pinch of salt

First make the pastry. Put the flour, ground almonds and baking powder into a bowl with a pinch of salt. Add the butter and rub it in until you have a mixture that resembles fine breadcrumbs. Add the egg, then just enough milk to bind everything together into a soft dough. Make sure the dough isn't crumbly, as this will make it harder to roll.

Wrap the dough and chill it for about half an hour to firm it up a little – don't leave it for much longer as you don't want it too firm.

To make the filling, put the raisins in a small saucepan and cover with 100ml of the Marsala. Bring to the boil, then simmer until the raisins have absorbed all the liquid. Remove the pan from the heat and leave the raisins to cool.

Put the cooled raisins in a food processor and pulse until they have broken down. Add the figs and continue to process until they have formed a thick paste. Transfer this to a bowl and add the remaining ingredients, including the rest of the Marsala and a generous pinch of salt. Mix thoroughly. The easiest way to do this is to knead the mixture with your hands until it starts to firm up. Chill the paste for at least half an hour – this will make it easier to handle when you assemble the biscuits. Line 2 baking trays with baking parchment.

Remove the pastry from the fridge and cut it into 2 even pieces. Roll each piece out into a rectangle measuring about 20 x 25cm. Cut each rectangle in half, lengthways.

Divide the fig paste into 4 even pieces and roll each piece into a log the length of the pastry rectangles. Place a log in a line down the centre of a pastry rectangle, lengthways, then bring one of the long sides up and over the filling so the edges meet and slightly overlap. Gently seal and roll over to make sure there aren't any cracks. Repeat with the remaining filling and pastry. Chill the logs for another half an hour – this will make them much easier to slice cleanly.

When you are ready to bake the fig rolls, preheat the oven to 180°C/Fan 160°C/Gas 4. Remove the logs from the fridge and cut each of them into 8 pieces. Arrange these on the baking trays and bake for 20–25 minutes until lightly golden. Remove from the oven and place on a wire rack to cool down. Store in an airtight tin.

CRANBERRY & PISTACHIO BISCOTTI

Cranberries and green pistachios give these biscotti a festive feel. They're just the thing for packing into a pretty box as a Christmas gift for someone special. And at any time of year, it's nice to have some of these in a jar next to your coffee machine.

Makes about 30

100g dried cranberries
up to 125ml Marsala
275g plain flour
1 tsp baking powder
1 tsp mixed spice
½ tsp ground allspice
pinch of salt
125g golden caster sugar
50g light brown soft sugar
zest of 1 mandarin or
    clementine (optional)
100g pistachio halves
2 eggs

Put the cranberries in a small saucepan and cover with 100ml of the Marsala. Bring to the boil, then remove the pan from the heat and leave the cranberries to swell and absorb most of the liquid. When cool, strain and reserve any liquid left in the saucepan.

Preheat the oven to 180°C/Fan 160°C/Gas 4 and line 2 baking trays with baking parchment.

Put the flour, baking powder and spices in a bowl with a generous pinch of salt. Add the sugars, zest, if using, the pistachio halves and the drained cranberries. Beat in the eggs, then add any reserved liquid from soaking the cranberries plus just enough Marsala to bind everything together into a fairly firm dough. Add the Marsala a tablespoon at a time, being careful not to add too much, as you don't want a sticky dough.

Divide the dough into 2 even pieces and roll them into logs of about 5cm in diameter and 20cm long. Place the logs on a baking tray and flatten them slightly, then bake for 25–30 minutes. These biscotti will take on a little more colour than usual because of the darker sugar and the Marsala and should be golden brown and firm to the touch.

Remove the biscotti from the oven and reduce the oven temperature to 150°C/Fan 130°C/Gas 2. When the logs are cool enough to handle, cut them into slices – you should get about 15 from each log. Arrange the biscotti over both baking trays and put them back in the oven. Bake for a further 20–25 minutes, turning them over halfway through, until they are hardened round the edges and firming up in the middle.

Remove from the oven and leave to cool – the biscotti will continue to harden. Store in an airtight tin. They should keep for a couple of weeks.

LANGUES DE CHAT BISCUITS

The English name for these is cat's tongues but the French sounds more exciting! They are lovely light biscuits that are perfect served alongside ice cream, sorbet or mousse or just with a cup of good coffee. This method of weighing the egg whites, then using the same amounts of butter, sugar and flour works really well and results in a very nice textured biscuit. We like the candied fennel seed topping but keep them plain if you prefer or add lavender, grated citrus zest or candied zest.

Makes 24–30

2 egg whites
up to 80g butter, softened
up to 80g icing sugar
up to 80g plain flour
zest of 1 lemon
pinch of salt

Candied fennel seeds
(optional)

2 tbsp granulated sugar
3 tbsp fennel seeds
pinch of salt

First make the candied fennel seeds, if using. Put the sugar in a saucepan with 2 tablespoons of water and slowly heat until the sugar has dissolved. Continue to simmer until the liquid turns syrupy, then add the fennel seeds and salt. Stir constantly over a medium heat. The sugar syrup will eventually reduce down to a thick, sticky syrup around the seeds and caramelise slightly, then it will suddenly go dry and powdery, which is what you want. As soon as this happens, remove the pan from the heat and transfer the seeds to a bowl to cool.

Line 2 baking sheets with baking parchment. Weigh the egg whites – each one will probably weigh 30–40g so 60–80g in total – then weigh out exactly the same amounts of butter, sugar and plain flour.

Put the butter and sugar in a bowl with the lemon zest and beat until well combined. Don't worry about increasing the volume too much, as you don't want to add a lot of air to the mixture. Beat in the flour, along with a pinch of salt, then lightly whisk the egg whites in a separate bowl and add these too. You should have a soft, spoonable batter.

Put a 1cm nozzle in a piping bag and spoon in the batter. Carefully pipe 7–8cm lengths of the batter on to the baking trays, making sure they are well spaced out. You should get a couple of rows per baking tray, probably 24–30 biscuits in all.

Put the baking trays in the fridge for at least half an hour until the batter is chilled and firm to the touch.

Preheat the oven to 180°C/Fan 160°C/Gas 4. Sprinkle the biscuits with some of the candied fennel seeds, if using. Put the baking trays in the oven and bake for 8–10 minutes until the biscuits are browned around the edges but still pale in the middle.

Remove the biscuits from the oven and immediately transfer them to wire racks. When they're cool, store them in an airtight container.

SEEDED RYE CRISPBREAD

Scandinavians have a whole crispbread culture and we were inspired to make these when we were filming in the Baltic. Our crispbread is thin, crisp and tasty, ideal to serve with dips or cheese or just as a crunchy snack. You can cut them into whatever size or shape you like, but we like the big rings and these definitely bake best with a hole cut in the middle. Experiment with the seed toppings to discover your favourite.

Makes 8 large or up to 40 small

300g wholemeal rye flour, plus extra for dusting
1 tsp salt
½ tsp baking powder
1 heaped tsp anise seeds (or any other seeds you prefer)
1 tsp honey
30g butter, softened

Topping (optional)

1 egg white
a mixture of seeds, such as caraway, anise, poppy and sesame

Put the flour in a bowl with the salt, baking powder, seeds, honey and butter. Mix thoroughly, then start adding up to 175ml of water while stirring, until you have a soft dough. Don't worry if the dough is a bit sticky, it will be fine once you start rolling.

Preheat the oven to 200°C/Fan 180°C/Gas 6. Turn the dough out on to a generously floured work surface and knead it lightly until smooth. Then roll the dough out thinly and prick it all over with a fork.

For classic 'ring' crispbreads, cut out rounds the size of a side or dinner plate. You should get 8 rounds the size of a small dinner plate from this amount of dough. You can leave them very rough and rustic looking, then cut a small hole in the middle as we have. If you prefer smaller crispbreads, this amount of dough should give you as many as 40.

For rectangular crispbreads, roll the dough into 4 pieces, each the size of a baking tray, then cut them free-form into long lengths.

If you want to add seeds, whisk the egg white with a tablespoon of water to break it up and brush it over the crispbreads. Sprinkle with your choice of seeds and press down lightly. The egg white will help the seeds stick.

Put the crispbreads on a baking tray and bake for about 10 minutes – a few minutes less for smaller sizes. Remove and leave to cool on a rack, then store in an airtight tin.

CHOCOLATE-COATED PECAN SHORTBREAD

We definitely like our shortbread with chocolate for a touch of extra luxury. Just coat half or cover the whole biscuit for a chocoholic feast. Totally epic and probably the most indulgent shortbread you'll ever have the pleasure to eat.

Makes about 24–32

225g plain flour, plus extra
　for dusting
75g fine cornmeal, plus extra
　for dusting
75g pecans, very finely chopped
200g butter, softened
75g caster sugar
pinch of salt

To finish

100g dark chocolate, broken up
2 tbsp maple syrup
2 tbsp milk
pinch of salt
50g pecans, very finely chopped

Put the flour, fine cornmeal, pecans, butter and sugar in a bowl and add a generous pinch of salt. Using a spoon or electric beaters, beat together until the ingredients come together into a soft dough.

Lightly flour your work surface. Roll out the dough to a thickness of 1cm, then cut it into 5cm rounds. Dust a couple of baking trays with cornmeal and place the biscuits on top. Place them in the fridge for at least half an hour to chill and firm up.

Preheat the oven to 150°C/Fan 130°C/Gas 2. Remove the biscuits from the fridge and bake them for 25–30 minutes until lightly browned on the underside and just starting to change colour on top. Remove them from the oven and leave to cool.

For the chocolate topping, put the chocolate in a bowl with the maple syrup, milk and salt. Set the bowl over a pan of gently simmering water and stir until the chocolate has melted and the mixture is smooth and glossy.

Use a spatula to smear chocolate over half of the top of each biscuit and sprinkle over some chopped pecans. Leave to cool until the chocolate hardens, then store in an airtight tin.

READ

SIMPLE BASIC BREAD

We wanted to give you a really good everyday bread recipe that works with any type of flour – white, wholemeal, granary or spelt – and this is it. Try a mix of spelt and rye, for example, and add some seeds as well, if you like, for extra texture. A useful tip is to use the water you've boiled potatoes in for the liquid – it makes for an extra-good texture.

Makes 1 loaf

500g strong bread flour, any sort, plus extra for dusting
7g fast-acting yeast
8g salt
1 tbsp sugar or honey or malt extract
about 300ml tepid water

Put the flour in a large bowl and mix in the yeast. Add the salt and the sugar, honey or malt extract. Slowly work in the tepid water until you have a fairly sticky dough. If you are using wholemeal or granary flour, you will probably need more water – up to 350ml. Just make sure that the dough is quite soft and not at all floury looking.

Cover the bowl with a damp tea towel and leave to stand for half an hour. The gluten will start to react during this time, making kneading easier. Turn the dough out on to a floured surface and knead until it is smooth and elastic. A simple way of telling whether it is ready is to apply the windowpane test: very gently pull the dough apart and it should stretch to form a very thin membrane that you can almost see through, before breaking.

Put the dough back in the bowl and cover it with a damp tea towel. Leave to stand for a couple of hours until doubled in size.

Knock back the dough until it deflates, then give it another quick knead. For a really good textured loaf, pat the dough out into an oblong the length of a large (900g) loaf tin. Then roll it up, starting with one of the longer sides, as tightly as you can and turn the short sides over. Press it firmly into your loaf tin and cover again with a damp tea towel. Leave to rise again.

You can also make a free-form loaf. After the first rise, turn the dough out on to a floured surface and knead it into a tight round or oval shape. Place the dough on a lined or floured baking tray and cover as above.

Preheat the oven to its highest setting.

When the dough has risen and has a well-rounded, springy dome, put it in the oven and bake for about 25 minutes until it has a crisp, well browned exterior and a hollow-sounding bottom. If you feel the base of the loaf needs crisping up, remove it from the tin and put it back in the oven for a further 5 minutes.

Cover the bread with a tea towel and leave it to cool to maintain a perfect crisp, but not too hard, crust. A free-form loaf will take the same amount of time to bake. If you'd like to make simple bread rolls, have a look at the recipe on page 263.

CHEESE & CHORIZO TEAR-&-SHARE BUNS

These deliciously savoury buns make a great dish for a picnic or a buffet – or just to enjoy with a bowl of soup for your supper. They look good and with the hit of chorizo, they taste even better. Naughty but nice!

Makes 8–10

500g strong white flour,
  plus extra for dusting
7g fast-acting yeast
1 tsp salt
1 tsp sugar or honey
2 tbsp olive oil
300ml tepid water
75g sliced hot chorizo,
  shredded
1 tsp dried thyme
50g Cheddar or Gouda,
  grated, plus another 50g
  for sprinkling
2 tbsp finely snipped chives

Glaze

2 tbsp olive oil
2 garlic cloves, crushed
½ tsp dried oregano
2 tbsp finely snipped chives

Line a 28cm cake tin or a roasting tin with greaseproof paper.

To make the dough, put the flour and yeast in a bowl and stir, then add the salt and the sugar or honey. Drizzle in the olive oil, then the water and mix to form a dough. Add the chorizo, thyme, 50g of the cheese and the chives. Knead the dough in the bowl for a minute or so to work the additions in a little, then knead on a floured surface until the dough is smooth. Put the dough back in the bowl, cover with a damp tea towel and leave to rest somewhere warm for 1½–2 hours, until doubled in size.

Preheat the oven to 220°C/Fan 200°C/Gas 7. Knock back the dough and divide it into 8–10 evenly sized pieces. Knead and shape these into balls, then arrange the balls in the prepared tin, slightly spacing them apart – they will meet as they prove again. Cover with a damp tea towel and leave to rise for another 20–30 minutes until they have risen and are squashing together.

Warm the oil and garlic in a pan over a low heat for a few minutes, then stir in the oregano and chives. Brush the mixture very gently over the buns, then sprinkle over the remaining cheese.

Bake in the preheated oven for 20–25 minutes until cooked through and a deep golden brown. Serve warm from the oven or leave to cool.

CHEAT'S SOURDOUGH

This is made with a yeast-based starter, known as a poolish. This was a method brought to France by Polish bakers in the 19th century and the great advantage is that there's no need to knead – the texture comes from the folding of the dough. Also, you don't have to worry about keeping a starter alive for weeks on end. Great with a ploughman's.

Makes 6

Poolish
150g strong white flour
150g tepid water
large pinch of fast-acting yeast

Dough
300g strong bread flour (white or wholemeal), plus extra for dusting
100g rye flour
100g mixed seeds, such as pumpkin, sunflower, sesame or milled flax (optional)
10g salt
½ tsp fast-acting yeast
1 tbsp honey
275–300ml tepid water

The day before you want to bake the bread, mix the poolish ingredients together in a small bowl. They will form a dough that looks like a thick paste. Cover and leave to stand overnight – you should find that the poolish will have increased in volume and will have a spongy, bubbly texture.

Put the bread flour, rye flour, seeds, if using, and salt in a large bowl and mix thoroughly. Add the yeast and honey and all of the poolish, then add enough of the water to make quite a wet, sticky dough.

Cover the bowl with a damp tea towel and then leave the dough to rest for 30 minutes. Next, stretch and fold the dough. This is very easy to do – simply take the top edge of the dough with both hands, stretch it upwards as far as you can without it breaking, then fold it over the unstretched dough. Then turn the bowl 90 degrees and repeat. Do this twice more until you have gone full circle. The dough will feel tighter with every fold. Repeat this process after another 30 minutes, and again 30 minutes after that.

After your last stretch and fold, leave for another 30 minutes, then turn the dough out on to a lightly floured surface. Stretch and fold it over one last time, again going full circle – when you flip over the bread it should be in quite a tight ball. Tighten it up a little more if necessary by tucking and turning the dough a few times, then place it on a baking tray. Cover with a damp tea towel and leave it to rise again.

Preheat the oven to 220°C/Fan 200°C/Gas 7. When the bread has risen again, test it to make sure it is ready – if you press it lightly with your finger, the indentation should slowly disappear. Bake in the oven for 25–30 minutes until the loaf is well browned and sounds hollow when you tap the bottom. For a softer crust, cover with a tea towel as it cools.

BRIOCHE BURGER BUNS

As you know, we love our burgers and we think it's worth getting the buns just right for completing the feast. We use a slightly simpler method than for the usual brioche – it's easier and still has really good results.

Makes 12 buns

250ml whole milk
75g butter
2 eggs, beaten, 1 tbsp reserved
600g strong white flour, plus extra for dusting
8g fast-acting yeast
25g caster sugar
1 tsp salt

Put the milk in a saucepan and heat until it is at blood temperature. Remove it from the heat and add the butter – the heat from the milk should be just enough to melt the butter completely. Leave to cool to room temperature, then beat in the eggs, setting aside a tablespoon of egg for later.

Put the flour into a bowl with the yeast and the sugar. Stir, then add the salt. Gradually work in the milk mixture until you have a very sticky, ragged dough. Knead until it becomes smooth – it's likely to be slightly tacky still. Cover with a damp tea towel and leave to prove until it has doubled in size.

Line 2 baking trays with baking parchment. Lightly flour your work surface.

Turn out the dough and knock it back, then divide it into 12 evenly sized pieces. Knead each piece into a smooth ball and place them on the baking trays, making sure they are well-spaced apart. Cover with a damp tea towel and leave to prove for a second time.

Preheat the oven to 180°C/Fan 160°C/Gas 4. When the buns have doubled in size again, remove the tea towel. Mix the reserved egg with a tablespoon of water and carefully brush the buns with the mixture. Be gentle, as the skin of the dough will be soft and tender.

Bake in the preheated oven for 20–25 minutes until the buns have risen into perfect domes and are a rich golden brown colour. Remove them from the oven and leave to cool.

IRISH SODA BREAD

With no yeast and no rising time, this is a quick and simple bread to make. If you get your skates on, it can be ready and on the table within the hour. Give us a slice of this, warm from the oven and spread with lashings of butter, and we're in heaven. Whenever we cook soda bread we wonder why we don't make it more often.

Makes 1 loaf

300g strong white flour,
    plus extra for dusting
200g strong wholemeal flour
1 tsp bicarbonate of soda
1½ tsp salt
1 tbsp malt extract
1 tbsp black treacle
up to 400ml buttermilk
2 tbsp porridge oats

Preheat the oven to 220°C/Fan 200°C/Gas 7.

Put the flours in a large bowl and mix in the bicarbonate of soda and salt.

Put the malt extract and treacle into a jug and add 100ml of the buttermilk. Whisk to combine and drizzle this into the flour mixture. Gradually work in the rest of the buttermilk until you have a fairly firm, slightly sticky dough. You may not need to add all of the buttermilk.

Turn the dough out on to a floured surface and shape it into a ball – this might be tricky if your dough is very sticky, but wetting your hands with cold water will help.

Sprinkle some flour over a baking tray, then place the dough on top. Cut a cross in the dough – it needs to be deep, almost to the base. Sprinkle the oats over the top.

Bake for 10 minutes, then reduce the oven temperature to 180°C/Fan 160°C/Gas 4. Continue to bake for up to 30 minutes or until the bread is well risen and browned. If it seems a little soft on the base, you can flip it over and bake it for another 10 minutes upside down.

Leave the bread to cool slightly on a wire rack. This is best eaten warm on the day it's made, but can be stored in an airtight container and it toasts well.

BABKA

Like a cake crossed with bread, babka is made with a wonderful enriched dough and a chocolate filling. We have to say, a stand mixer does make life much easier with this one.

Makes 1 loaf

Dough

75g butter, softened, plus
   extra for greasing
150ml whole milk
2 eggs
1 tsp vanilla extract
175g plain flour, plus extra
   for dusting
150g strong white flour
5g fast-acting yeast
50g light brown soft sugar
½ tsp salt

Chocolate filling

75g butter
75g light brown soft sugar
100g dark chocolate, broken up
2 tbsp cocoa powder
½ tsp vanilla extract
75g pecans, finely chopped
   (optional)

Butter a large (900g) loaf tin and line it with baking parchment. Put the milk in a pan and heat until just warm – about blood temperature. Remove the pan from the heat and beat in the eggs and vanilla.

Put the flours in a bowl, stir in the yeast and sugar, then add the salt. Gradually work in the milk and egg mixture to make a very wet, sticky, stretchy dough. If you're using a stand mixer, the dough will mix much better with the paddle/ beater attachment rather than with the dough hook.

Add the butter, a tablespoon at a time, making sure you work it in completely before adding the next tablespoon. When you have worked in all the butter, knead the dough until it is still very soft but smooth and much less sticky. If using a stand mixer, change to a dough hook for this stage. Cover with a damp tea towel and leave the dough to double in size. This will take at least 2 hours.

While the dough is proving, make the chocolate filling. Heat the butter and sugar together in a small pan. When the butter has melted and the sugar has dissolved, add the chocolate, cocoa powder and vanilla extract. Stir over a very low heat until everything is well combined into a paste. The paste might be slightly grainy but that's fine. Remove from the heat and leave to cool.

Generously flour a work surface and tip the dough on to it. It will still be very soft. Press it out into a large rectangle measuring about 25–30 x 50–60cm.

Spread the chocolate paste over the dough, going right to the edges, then sprinkle with the pecans, if using. Roll the dough up as tightly as you can, starting from one of the longest sides. Next, cut through the roll, lengthways, leaving a few centimetres still joined at one end. Now, twist the 2 lengths together. To start, just fold one length over the other, then when you get further down the length you can hold both ends and twist the lengths round one another. You will end up with a long 2-stranded plait – it will have stretched slightly during this process.

Drape the plait of dough into your loaf tin, lowering it in from one short end to the next in a zigzag until you have used it all up – you will end up with 3 or 4 layers. Cover with a damp tea towel and leave to prove again.

Preheat the oven to 180°C/Fan 160°C/Gas 4. Check the dough after half an hour. When it is ready for baking, it will still look quite firm, and an indentation made with your finger should slowly disappear.

Bake in the oven for 25 minutes, then cover the top with foil to prevent burning. Continue to bake for a further 20–25 minutes until the babka sounds hollow when tapped. Turn it out on to a wire rack to cool before slicing.

HOKKAIDO MILK BREAD

The ultimate Japanese sandwich loaf – we used this on a TV show with some very special beef but it's just as good with ham and cheese or some butter and jam. The dough can be a bit tricky, but it's easy to do in a stand mixer with a dough hook.

Makes 1 loaf

Starter
30g strong white bread flour
75g whole milk
pinch of salt

Dough
350g strong white bread flour,
    plus extra for dusting
50g granulated sugar
7g fast-acting yeast
1 tbsp milk powder
1 tsp salt
125ml whole milk
1 egg, beaten
60g butter, softened, plus extra
    for greasing
double cream or melted butter,
    for brushing

First make the starter. Put the flour, milk and 75ml of water in a small saucepan with a pinch of salt. Stir over a medium heat, whisking constantly, until the mixture starts to thicken, then keep whisking until it has the texture of a very thick béchamel sauce or mashed potato. Transfer it to a bowl and cover, then leave to cool to room temperature.

Put the 350g of flour, the sugar, yeast, milk powder and salt in the bowl of a stand mixer or a food processor with a dough hook. Stir to combine. Gradually beat in the milk and egg, followed by the starter. The dough will be very soft and straggly, but do not be tempted to add more flour. Mix with the dough hook until the dough starts to come together, then add the butter. Continue to mix until the butter is completely combined with the dough, then continue kneading with the dough hook until the dough is smooth. It will still be very soft but shouldn't be sticky.

Put the dough back in the bowl and cover with a damp tea towel. Leave it somewhere warm to prove for an hour or so or until doubled in size. You can also prove it overnight in the fridge if you prefer – this will give you a firmer dough which is easier to work with.

When you are ready to shape the dough, generously butter a large loaf tin and dust it with flour.

Turn the dough out and cut it into 4 equal pieces. Turn a piece out on to a floured surface and roll it into a diamond shape – the sides should measure about 20–21cm. Take the left and right corners and fold them into the dough so that they meet in the middle. Roll up the dough as tightly as you can and drop it into the tin. Repeat with the other 3 pieces – you should find that the 4 rolls fit snugly next to each other in the loaf tin.

Cover again and leave to prove for another 45 minutes to an hour until the dough is well risen and springy to touch. The sections will come together as a loaf. Preheat the oven to 180°C/Fan 160°C/Gas 4.

Brush the dough with the double cream or melted butter and bake in the oven for 35–40 minutes until the loaf is a rich golden brown. Cool on a wire rack and wait until completely cool before slicing.

OUR NORTHERN BAGUETTE

Dave: I invented this during lockdown. My Romanian mother-in-law was living with us and I was baking bread on a daily basis. But after a while I realised that she was too polite to say she didn't like my crusty loaves, so I came up with this idea which is halfway between a baguette and a submarine roll. It really works with your favourite filling or as something to have on the table for mopping up a good sauce, northern style.

Makes 8

250ml whole milk
3 tbsp olive oil
1 egg, beaten, 1 tbsp
    reserved
350g strong white bread flour,
    plus extra for dusting
150g light rye flour
7g fast-acting yeast
1 tsp caster sugar
1 tsp salt
fine semolina, for dusting
    and sprinkling

Put the milk in a saucepan and heat very gently just to take the fridge-chill off it. Add the olive oil and most of the beaten egg, setting a tablespoon of egg aside for later.

Put the flours in a bowl with the yeast and sugar. Give everything a quick stir, then add the salt. Gradually work in the milk mixture until you have a fairly firm, sticky dough, then leave to stand for half an hour.

Knead the dough on a floured surface until it is smooth and no longer sticky. It should also pass the windowpane test – very gently pull the dough apart and it should stretch to form a very thin membrane that you can almost see through, before breaking. Cover with a damp tea towel and leave to prove until doubled in size – this will take at least an hour.

Dust a couple of baking trays with semolina.

Knock back the dough and cut it into 8 even pieces. Roll or squeeze each piece out into baguette lengths. For fairly short baguettes, the width of a baking tray, they will need to be about 4cm in diameter. For much skinnier baguettes, the length of a baking tray, they will be about 2cm in diameter. And if you want more of a baguette look, feel free to cut a few slashes across the top of each one.

Cover the baguettes with a damp tea towel again and leave to prove for another hour until they have doubled in size again.

Preheat the oven to 210°C/Fan 190°C/Gas 6½. Mix the reserved egg with a tablespoon of water and carefully brush the mixture over the baguettes. Sprinkle with more semolina.

Put a roasting tin in the base of the oven. Put the baking trays in the oven, then add about 600ml of freshly boiled water to the roasting tin. It will create a lot of steam which will help the baguettes develop a nice crust.

Bake in the oven for 10–12 minutes for the thin baguettes or 15–18 minutes for the wider ones. Remove the baguettes from the oven when they are a rich, glossy brown.

CINNAMON ROLLS

There's nothing as tempting as the smell of cinnamon rolls baking in the oven! We've suggested a couple of methods of cooking these. Baking them on a tray in the usual way gives a nice soft roll, but you can also pop them into muffin tins for a roll with more crust. Also, once the rolls are on the tray or in the muffin tin, you can leave them in the fridge overnight. In the morning, take them out as soon as you get up, let them warm and rise for about 45 minutes, then bake them ready for a luxurious brunch.

Makes 12

Dough
250g plain flour, plus extra
    for dusting
250g strong white flour
50g caster sugar
7g fast-acting yeast
1 tsp ground cinnamon
¼ tsp ground cloves
¼ tsp ground cardamom
½ tsp salt
225ml whole milk
100g butter, softened
2 eggs, beaten, 1 tbsp reserved

Filling
150g butter, softened
125g light brown soft sugar
1 tbsp ground cinnamon
pinch of salt

Topping
50g caster sugar
1 tbsp cinnamon

Mix the plain flour and strong flour together in a bowl with the sugar, yeast and spices, then add the salt.

Put the milk in a saucepan and heat very gently to just above blood temperature. Add the butter – the milk should be just warm enough to melt it. Beat in the eggs, setting a tablespoon of egg aside for later.

Pour the milk mixture into the bowl with the flours and mix until you have a soft, sticky dough. Turn the dough out on to a floured work surface and knead until the mixture is no longer sticky but smooth and elastic. It should pass the windowpane test – very gently pull the dough apart and it should stretch to form a thin membrane that you can almost see through, before breaking.

Put the dough back in the bowl and cover with a damp tea towel, then leave it somewhere warm to rise until it has doubled in size. To check, press the dough with your finger – if the indentation slowly disappears, it's ready.

For the filling, mix the butter, sugar and cinnamon together with a generous pinch of salt.

Dust your work surface with flour and turn the dough out. Knock it back and shape it into a rectangle of about 35 x 25cm. Spread the filling over the dough as evenly as possible, then roll it up tightly from the longest edge. Cut it into 12 pieces.

Line a baking tray with baking parchment and place the rolls on it, spacing them well apart. As they prove and bake, they will expand and meet each other. Alternatively, take a 12-hole muffin tin and drop a roll into each hole – they will rise and push the centre up, giving them more of a raised swirl. Cover the rolls with a damp tea towel and leave them to prove for half an hour or so.

Preheat the oven to 200°C/Fan 180°C/Gas 6. Mix the reserved egg with a tablespoon of water and brush this over the rolls. Mix the sugar and cinnamon together and sprinkle half of it over the rolls. Leave them to stand for a few minutes – some of the sugar will be absorbed by the egg – and then sprinkle over the rest.

Bake the rolls in the preheated oven for about 25 minutes until they are a rich brown and well risen. Remove from the oven and eat while they are still warm to enjoy them at their best.

SAFFRON BUNS

We're fascinated at how often you find special baking traditions and culinary gems in different parts of the country and these are a good example. Saffron has long been a popular spice in Cornwall – some say from the days of trading in tin – and these buns are a popular local delicacy. They smell amazing!

Makes 10

1 large pinch of saffron threads
250ml whole milk
75g clotted or double cream
50g butter, softened
500g plain flour, plus extra
   for dusting
7g fast-acting yeast
50g caster sugar
100g currants
25g candied citrus peel,
   finely chopped (optional)
1 tsp salt

Put the saffron in a dry frying pan and heat gently, stirring constantly, until the aroma intensifies and the threads crisp up. Remove the pan from the heat and crush the threads with the back of a wooden spoon or spatula – you will find that they break up quickly and easily.

Put the saffron in a saucepan with the milk. Place over a low heat and bring to just below boiling point, then remove the pan from the heat and add the clotted or double cream and the butter. Leave until the butter has melted and the mixture has cooled to tepid.

Put the flour in a bowl and add the yeast, sugar, currants and citrus peel, if using. Give everything a quick stir, then add the salt. Gradually work in the milk and saffron mixture until you have a soft, sticky dough. Cover with a damp tea towel and leave for 20 minutes.

Turn the dough out on to a floured surface and knead for about 10 minutes until it is soft and smooth and passes the windowpane test – very gently pull the dough apart and it should stretch to form a very thin membrane that you can almost see through, before breaking. If you like, you can use the dough hook on a stand or an electric mixer.

Cover the dough with a damp tea towel and leave it somewhere warm to prove. Line a baking tray with baking parchment. When the dough has doubled in size, knock it back gently and divide it into 10 pieces.

Knead each piece gently into a ball and place them on the baking tray, well-spaced apart. Cover with a damp tea towel and leave to prove again.

Preheat the oven to 200°C/Fan 180°C/Gas 6. When the buns are well risen, bake them for about 20 minutes until firm and hollow sounding. Serve them warm from the oven or cold – they will keep for several days in an airtight tin.

SESAME BAGELS

Everyone loves a bagel and these are fun to make. The malt extract gives them a beautiful colour and its sweetness means you don't have to add any sugar. You do need to give the dough some welly though – but it's all good exercise! It might feel like a leap of faith to boil dough but that's what gives the bagel its chew.

Makes 8

500g strong white flour
5g fast-acting yeast
2 scant tsp salt
1 tbsp malt extract
100ml just-boiled water
160ml tepid water

To boil

1 tsp salt
1 tsp bicarbonate of soda
1 tbsp malt extract

To glaze

1 egg white, well beaten
2 tbsp sesame seeds
  (or poppy or nigella seeds)

Put the flour into a large bowl. Add the yeast and stir, then add the salt. Put the malt extract into a measuring jug, add the just-boiled water and stir to dissolve the malt extract. Then add the tepid water to the jug.

Gradually mix the liquid into the dry ingredients. The dough can be quite hard to work, unless you have a stand mixer, but try to resist adding any more water. Keep kneading until the dough is softer and smooth, then cover with a damp tea towel and leave for 1–2 hours until doubled in size.

Check the dough regularly – it should have risen but not puffed up. To check if it has risen enough, gently press it with your finger – it should spring back slowly. Cut the dough into 8 equal pieces and form them into tight balls. To form rings, push a finger into the centre of each ball, then add a finger from your other hand and roll your fingers over one another until the hole gets bigger and stretches the bagel.

Place the bagels on a baking tray lined with baking parchment and cover them with a damp tea towel again. Leave to prove for another 30 minutes.

Preheat the oven to its highest temperature and bring a large saucepan of water to the boil. When the water is boiling, add the salt and the bicarbonate of soda – the water will foam up. When the foam has subsided, add the malt extract and stir until it has dissolved.

Add the bagels to the boiling water, 2 or 3 at a time. Boil for 30 seconds on each side, then remove and place them back on the lined baking tray. Brush them with the egg white and sprinkle with seeds. Bake in the oven for 15–20 minutes until golden brown and hollow sounding when tapped.

OLIVE BREAD ROLLS

Bread made with olive oil has a lovely soft texture and a beautiful flavour. These rolls are great for making fabulous Mediterranean-inspired sandwiches with ingredients like halloumi and tomatoes or Dave's favourite – tuna mayo. You can experiment with this recipe and add stuffed olives instead of plain, or some capers and lemon zest.

Makes 12

500g strong white flour,
    plus extra for dusting
7g fast-acting yeast
8g salt
75g pitted olives, (black
    or green), sliced
100ml olive oil
275ml tepid water

Put the flour in a bowl with the yeast. Give it a quick stir, then add the salt and the olives. Pour in the olive oil, then gradually add the water, mixing as you go, until you have a fairly soft, sticky dough. Leave it to stand, covered with a damp tea towel, for 30 minutes.

Turn the dough out on to a floured work surface and knead until it is smooth and not tacky. Check it with the windowpane test – very gently pull the dough apart and it should stretch to form a very thin membrane that you can almost see through, before breaking.

Put the dough back in the bowl, cover with a damp tea towel and leave somewhere warm for about 2 hours or until doubled in size.

Turn the bread dough out on to the floured work surface again. Cut it into 12 even pieces (weigh them if you like), then shape them into rounds or oblongs. Place them on a large baking tray lined with baking parchment or, if you want to ensure they don't touch once they've risen, spread them over 2 baking trays.

Cover with a damp tea towel and leave to prove for another 30 minutes to an hour, until they have doubled in size again. Preheat the oven to 220°C/ Fan 200°C/Gas 7.

Slash down the centre of each roll, then bake them in the oven for about 20 minutes until well browned with a hard crust. If you like a softer crust, cover the rolls with a tea towel while they cool.

HERB & TOMATO FOCACCIA

We first cooked this in a street in Venice many years ago and this is our new, improved version. It's a traditional Italian bread that's fairly flat in shape and usually made in a baking tin. We've flavoured ours with herbs, garlic and tomatoes, but you might like to experiment with other toppings, such as olives. It makes a nice side dish for mopping up sauces and is also good served with extra virgin olive oil and balsamic vinegar for dipping. By the way, 00 flour is a finely ground flour that's preferred in Italy for pizzas and the like. If you don't have any, use 600g of strong white instead.

Serves 4–6

300g strong white flour
300g 00 flour
8g fast-acting yeast
10g salt
2 tsp runny honey
75ml olive oil, plus more
    for oiling
400ml tepid water

To finish

30ml olive oil
2 garlic cloves, finely sliced
16 basil leaves and their stems,
    separated
16 cherry tomatoes
1 tsp dried rosemary
1 tsp sea salt

Put the flours in a bowl and sprinkle in the yeast. Mix thoroughly, then add the salt. Drizzle in the honey and oil, then add the water to make a fairly soft, sticky dough. Turn the dough out on to a well-oiled work surface (oil works better than flour with a wetter dough like this) and knead until it's smooth and no longer sticky. Use a stand mixer if you prefer.

Oil a large bowl, put the dough in it and cover. Leave the dough in the fridge to rise overnight, or put it somewhere warm for 2–3 hours until it has puffed up and doubled in size.

If you have left your dough in the fridge overnight, remove it an hour or so before you want to bake the bread. Knock back the dough. Generously oil a 30 x 20cm baking tin and scrape the dough into it. Pull the dough into a rectangle but don't worry too much if it doesn't completely fill the tin – it will move into every available space as it rises again. Cover and leave to rise for another 30 minutes to an hour until it has doubled in size.

Preheat the oven to 220°C/Fan 200°C/Gas 7. Put the 30ml of olive oil in a small saucepan with the garlic and the basil stems. Heat very gently for a few minutes, then remove from the heat. Leave to infuse and cool to room temperature, then strain. Whisk the oil with 30ml of water until the mixture completely emulsifies.

Press your fingertips all over the dough to create a dimpled effect. Wrap each cherry tomato in a basil leaf and poke it into the dough. Pour the oil and water mixture over the top of the focaccia, using a brush to spread it evenly, then sprinkle with the rosemary and sea salt. Bake in the oven for 25–30 minutes until it's a light golden brown. Remove from the tin and leave to cool on a wire rack.

LAHMACUN

We first became addicted to these flatbreads when filming in Turkey in 2007 and we sampled them everywhere, from street stalls to restaurants. Topped with a delicious mixture of minced meat and spices, they make a great change from pizza. Serve with a salad for supper or you could cut them into smaller pieces to serve as a snack or appetiser.

Makes 4

Dough
250g strong white flour,
    plus extra for dusting
1 tsp fast-acting yeast
½ tsp caster sugar
1 tsp salt
1 tbsp olive oil
up to 150ml tepid water

Topping
1 tbsp olive oil
2 tbsp tomato purée
1 tsp Aleppo pepper flakes
    (pul biber), or sweet paprika
1 tsp ground cumin
½ tsp ground cinnamon
1 small onion, very finely
    chopped
½ green or red pepper, very
    finely chopped
2 garlic cloves, crushed or grated
small bunch of parsley, finely
    chopped
250g lean beef or lamb mince
salt and black pepper

To finish
zest of 1 lemon
1 small red onion, finely sliced
1 tbsp olive oil

To serve
sumac
lemon wedges

First make the dough. Put the flour in a bowl with the yeast and sugar. Mix to disperse the yeast, then add the salt. Drizzle in the olive oil, then up to 150ml of tepid water, until the dough comes together – it will be slightly sticky.

Turn the dough out on to a floured work surface and knead until it is smooth and elastic. Try the windowpane test – very gently pull the dough apart and it should stretch to form a very thin membrane that you can almost see through, before breaking. Put the dough back in the bowl and cover it with a damp tea towel, then leave it for about an hour until it is well risen.

To make the filling, put the olive oil, tomato purée and spices into a bowl with a generous amount of salt and pepper. Mix to combine, then stir in the onion, pepper, garlic, half the parsley and the beef or lamb. Mix again.

Preheat the oven to 220°C/Fan 200°C/Gas 7. Place a couple of baking trays in the oven to heat up.

To assemble the lahmacun, cut the dough into 4 equal pieces. On a floured work surface, roll or stretch out each piece of dough into rounds, making them as thin as you can – aim for a diameter of 20–25cm. Place each one on a piece of baking parchment.

Divide the filling by 4 and sprinkle it evenly over each round. Sprinkle over the zest. Toss the slices of onion in the olive oil, then arrange them over the filling. Keeping the lahmacun on the baking parchment, carefully slide them on to the heated baking trays. Bake for up to 10 minutes, until the dough is crisp around the edges and the topping is cooked through.

Sprinkle with sumac and the reserved parsley and serve with some lemon wedges on the side for squeezing over the top.

STUFFED FLATBREADS

Flavoured with lots of herbs and spices, these are completely delicious and you can get all the elements prepared in advance. Roasting the tomatoes for the sauce intensifies the flavour but if you don't have time, just finely chop raw tomatoes.

Makes 4

Flatbreads
250g strong white bread flour, plus extra for dusting
¼ tsp fast-acting yeast
1 tsp nigella seeds
75ml yoghurt
1 tbsp olive oil
100ml tepid water

Filling
75g cooked new potatoes, finely diced
3 spring onions, chopped
2 green chillies, finely diced
200g halloumi, coarsely grated
small bunch each of coriander and parsley, finely chopped, 2 tbsp of each reserved
3 large dill sprigs, finely chopped, 1 tsp reserved
1 tsp dried mint
1 tsp dried fenugreek leaf (optional)
½ tsp chilli flakes
½ tsp ground cumin
½ tsp ground coriander
salt and black pepper

Tomato and yoghurt sauce
150g ripe tomatoes, halved
1 tbsp olive oil
1 garlic clove, finely chopped
300g thick yoghurt
½ tsp chilli flakes
zest and juice of ½ lime

For brushing
50g butter
3 garlic cloves, thinly sliced

First make the flatbreads. Put the flour in a bowl with the yeast and nigella seeds. Stir to combine and then sprinkle in a teaspoon of salt. Mix the yoghurt and oil with the tepid water, then work this mixture into the dry ingredients to make a sticky dough.

Turn the dough out on to a floured work surface and knead until smooth and elastic. Put it back in the bowl and cover with a damp tea towel. Leave the dough to stand for about an hour until it has increased in size.

Put all the ingredients for the filling into a bowl with plenty of salt and pepper and mix thoroughly.

Preheat the oven to 200°C/Fan 180°C/Gas 6. Put the tomatoes for the sauce in a roasting tin and drizzle them with olive oil. Sprinkle with salt and pepper. Roast for 15–20 minutes until they start to char, then remove them from the oven and set them aside to cool.

Divide the dough into 4 equal pieces. Dust your work surface with flour and roll or press out each piece of dough as thinly as you can – it should be at least 20cm long and 15cm wide. Take a quarter of the filling and pile it on to one half of the dough. Press it down so it compacts, then fold the exposed dough over and seal the edges, making sure you get rid of any air pockets as you go. Lightly flatten the stuffed flatbreads a little with a rolling pin – if you like, you can also reshape them at this point into rounds or ovals.

Turn the oven up to 220°C/Fan 200°C/Gas 7. Place the flatbreads on a couple of baking trays. To prepare the mixture for brushing, melt the butter in a small frying pan and add the garlic and a large pinch of salt. Place over a very gentle heat and let the garlic soften in the butter. Watch it carefully and as soon as the garlic starts to colour, remove it from the pan with a slotted spoon and set it aside. Brush the flatbreads with half the butter. Place the flatbreads in the oven and bake for 15 minutes until well browned.

Finish the sauce. Put the finely chopped garlic in a bowl with the roasted tomatoes and all the remaining ingredients, including the herbs reserved from making the flatbread filling. Season with plenty of salt and pepper and leave the sauce to stand.

Remove the flatbreads from the oven and brush them with the remaining butter. Serve with the tomato and yoghurt sauce.

GLU

UTEN-
FREE

GLUTEN-FREE CRISPBREADS

These make a lovely little snack with some cheese or perhaps spread with butter and honey. Using all the different seeds means they are packed with nutrients and fibre too, so they're really good for you as well as tasty.

Makes 12–20

100g buckwheat or brown rice
   flour, plus extra for dusting
75g ground almonds
2 tbsp sunflower seeds
2 tbsp sesame seeds
2 tbsp milled flax seeds
2 tbsp pumpkin seeds
½ tsp salt
3 tbsp olive oil
2 egg whites, lightly whisked

Topping (optional)

1 tsp cumin seeds
25g hard cheese, such as
   Gouda, Gruyère, mature
   Cheddar or Parmesan, grated

Preheat the oven to 180°C/Fan 160°C/Gas 4. Line a large baking tray with baking parchment.

Put the flour, ground almonds and seeds in a bowl with the salt. Stir in the olive oil and egg whites, and mix until the dough starts to clump together. It will still be very floury – more like a crumble mixture – at this stage.

Add just enough water, about 1–2 tablespoons, to bring the mixture together, then knead lightly into a dough.

Lay a piece of baking parchment on your work surface – it will stay in place much better if the work surface is slightly damp. Dust the baking parchment with flour and place the ball of dough on top. Roll the dough out on the baking parchment into a rectangle to fit your baking tray. The dough should be quite thin – about 3mm.

Sprinkle the rolled-out dough with the cumin seeds, if using, pressing the seeds lightly into the dough. Add the cheese, if using, over the top and press that down too.

Score the dough into rectangles, cutting almost all the way through with a sharp knife or a pizza wheel – use a ruler to keep your lines straight. Scoring like this will make the dough easier to break into crackers once it has baked. You should get 12–20 crackers, depending on how large you want them.

Bake the crispbread in the oven for 15–20 minutes until golden brown and quite dry to the touch. Remove from the oven and leave to cool – the crispbread will continue to crisp up as it cools. Break along the score lines and store in an airtight container.

GLUTEN-FREE NAAN BREAD

We wanted to find something for our gluten-free friends to enjoy with their curries and we've been experimenting with different ideas. Using oil and yoghurt to make this dough works well and you don't need to add extras like xanthan gum. The dough does need careful handling but it firms up beautifully once cooked.

Makes 6

300g gluten-free flour, plus
    extra for dusting
1 tsp caster sugar
2 tsp gluten-free baking powder
1 tsp garlic powder
1 scant tsp salt
a few coriander sprigs,
    finely chopped
2 tbsp olive oil
125g plain yoghurt
1 egg, beaten

Topping

25g butter, melted
1 tsp nigella or sesame seeds

Preheat the oven to 220°C/Fan 200°C/Gas 7 and line 2 baking trays with baking parchment.

Put the flour, sugar, baking powder and garlic powder into a bowl with the salt. Stir to combine, then add the coriander, oil, yoghurt and egg. Mix until you have a fairly smooth dough.

Dust your work surface generously with flour. Divide the mixture into 6 pieces, then roll or pat them out into thin teardrop shapes. Try to make sure each one is about 5mm thick, no more.

Carefully transfer the naan breads to the baking trays – it's easiest to do this with a palette knife rather than by hand, as the dough can be quite fragile. Brush them with the melted butter and sprinkle them with nigella or sesame seeds. Bake in the oven for 15–18 minutes.

You can also cook these on the hob. Heat a pan (a cast-iron pan works best) until hot. Brush the naans with the butter and sprinkle them with seeds, as before, then cook them one at a time, flipping them over after 2 or 3 minutes, until cooked through and lightly charred in places. Keep the breads warm under a tea towel until all 6 are cooked.

These are best eaten immediately, but you can reheat them – sprinkle the breads with water and warm them through in a pan or put them in a hot oven for 5 minutes.

OATCAKES

Lots of shop-bought oatcakes contain wheat, so you might like to make your own, gluten-free version. Don't forget that you must use gluten-free flour for dusting your work surface. If you don't have any, cornflour is fine or just blitz some oats to the texture of flour in a food processor. Butter, lard or goose fat are traditional for oatcakes, but olive oil is fine too.

Makes 18

200g porridge oats
½ tsp gluten-free baking powder
½ tsp salt
30ml olive oil or melted
   butter, lard or goose fat
up to about 100ml hot water
gluten-free flour, for dusting

Preheat the oven to 200°C/Fan 180°C/Gas 6.

Put the porridge oats in a food processor and blitz them briefly until partially broken down into a rough, floury texture. Add the baking powder and salt. With the motor running, drizzle in the olive oil or whichever fat you are using, followed by as much of the water as necessary to form a slightly sticky dough.

Clump the dough together into a ball, then lightly dust your work surface with gluten-free flour. Roll out the dough until it is about 3–4mm thick, then cut it into 6cm rounds. Scrunch up any offcuts and re-roll. You do have to work fast as the oats absorb liquid very quickly and the mixture may become crumbly. If this does happen, wet your hands and reform the dough. You should get about 18 rounds.

Place the oatcakes on a baking tray – they don't need to be well spaced – and bake them for about 20 minutes. The oatcakes will not brown much and they will still be slightly soft when they come out of the oven, but they'll firm up nicely as they cool.

Leave the oatcakes to cool, then store in an airtight container.

GRAM FLOUR YORKSHIRES WITH CURRY SAUCE

Yorkshire puddings made with gram or chickpea flour are gluten-free without even trying and are really good to eat. These can be served with anything, but they are great with this curry sauce and perhaps a veggie curry like saag aloo on the side.

Serves 4–6

Batter

75g gram (chickpea) flour
75g cornflour
½ tsp turmeric (optional)
½ tsp salt
4 eggs
125ml whole milk
dripping, lard or olive oil

Curry sauce

1 tbsp coconut or olive oil
½ tsp nigella seeds (optional)
½ tsp cumin seeds (optional)
1 large onion, finely chopped
4 garlic cloves, finely chopped
   or grated
15g root ginger, finely grated
small bunch of coriander, stems
   and leaves separated, finely
   chopped
400g lamb or beef mince
1 tsp medium or hot chilli
   powder (according to taste)
1 tbsp mild curry powder
400g can of tomatoes
1 tbsp tamarind paste
½ tsp caster sugar
300ml beef, chicken
   or vegetable stock
salt and black pepper

To make the batter for the Yorkshire puddings, put both flours in a bowl with the turmeric, if using, and the salt. Whisk in the eggs. Mix the milk with 100ml of water, then whisk this into the batter until it has the consistency of thin single cream. Leave to stand for an hour.

Meanwhile, get the curry sauce started. Heat the oil in a saucepan and add the nigella and cumin seeds, if using. As soon as they start to pop, add the onion and sauté over a medium heat until softened. Add the garlic, ginger, coriander stems and lamb or beef mince and continue to cook until the meat has browned.

Stir in the chilli powder and curry powder, followed by the tomatoes, tamarind, sugar and stock. Season with plenty of salt and pepper. Bring to the boil, then turn down the heat and cover the pan. Simmer for 20 minutes, then remove the lid and continue to simmer for another 10–15 minutes to reduce the sauce down a bit.

Preheat the oven to 220°C/Fan 200°C/Gas 7. Put dollops of whichever fat you are using into the holes of a 12-hole muffin tin or a 6-hole Yorkshire pudding tin or just into a large roasting tin. Heat until smoking – this usually takes a good 10–15 minutes.

Pour the batter on to the fat, dividing it as evenly as possible between the tins if making individual puddings. Bake in the oven for 15–20 minutes for the small puddings or up to 25–30 minutes for the roasting tin version, until well risen and crisp around the sides.

Remove from the oven and serve immediately with the sauce. The puddings will keep and reheat well in the oven if necessary.

AMARETTO CHOCOLATE TORTE

This might be gluten-free but there's no stinting on anything else. With loads of chocolate and butter, it's decadently rich and luxuriously delicious. It's uncomplicated but tastes really special – just the thing to share with friends, whether they're gluten-free or not. Can we come round?

Makes about 12 slices

200g dark chocolate, broken
   into pieces
135g butter, diced
50g honey (a fragrant one
   like orange blossom)
50ml amaretto liqueur
75g golden caster sugar
3 eggs

To serve
double cream or clotted cream

Preheat the oven to 130°C/Fan 110°C/Gas 1. Line a 21cm round cake tin with baking parchment. If the tin is loose-based, wrap the outside in foil – the torte is baked in a water bath, so it's important to make sure it is watertight.

Put the chocolate, butter and honey in a heatproof bowl and place it over a pan of barely simmering water. Stir occasionally until everything has melted into a smooth, runny sauce. Add the amaretto and stir to combine.

In a separate bowl, whisk the sugar and eggs together until they have increased dramatically in volume and have a very mousse-like texture. Check the mixture is firm enough by drizzling a trail of it across the surface – it should only very slowly lose its shape.

Pour the chocolate mixture in around the edge of the egg and sugar mixture, then fold everything together – try to avoid losing too much of the volume. Use light delicate motions but make sure there are no streaks. You will end up with a dark, pourable batter.

Pour the batter into the prepared tin. Place the cake tin in a roasting tin and pour just-boiled water around it to come about halfway up the sides of the cake tin. It's safest to put the roasting tin in the oven first, then pull the oven shelf out just enough so you can pour in the boiling water.

Bake the torte for about 45–50 minutes until just set. You can tell it is about done if, when you lightly touch the surface, your finger comes away clean.

Remove the torte from the oven and leave it to rest in the tin for at least half an hour until cool. Turn it out and remove the baking parchment, then enjoy right away or leave it to chill in the fridge – the texture will become denser and fudgier. Nice served with cream.

CHESTNUT MADELEINES

These buttery little cakes are a real French classic and are easy to make. Traditionally, they are baked in special madeleine tins, which gives them their shell-like shape, but you could also make them in fairy cake tins if you like. This recipe uses chestnut flour, which is a great gluten-free option, and if you really want to push the boat out, drizzle some chestnut honey over them. Best eaten warm from the oven.

Make 24

100g butter, plus extra for
   brushing
100g golden caster sugar
2 eggs
pinch of salt
100g chestnut flour, plus extra
   for dusting
½ tsp gluten-free baking powder

Melt the butter in a small saucepan, then leave it to cool to blood temperature.

Whisk the sugar and eggs together with a pinch of salt, until frothy and aerated, but still fairly liquid. Whisk in the chestnut flour and baking powder, then the melted butter.

Cover and leave the mixture to chill in the fridge for at least an hour – or overnight if that's easier. This chilling time is important for making sure the cakes form the traditional madeleine 'hump'.

When you are ready to bake, preheat the oven to 180°C/Fan 160°C/Gas 4. Melt about 15g more butter and use it to brush the moulds in the madeleine tin or fairy cake tin. Dust the moulds with flour, then tap off the excess.

Spoon in the madeleine batter so the moulds are about two-thirds full. Bake in the oven for 8–10 minutes until golden brown and looking crisp around the edges. Turn the madeleines out on to a wire rack and aim to eat them within the hour.

If you need to cook your madeleines in 2 batches, cool the tin under cold water after baking the first batch and wash it. Then recoat with butter and flour and proceed as before with the remaining batter.

LEMON & ALMOND CAKE

Cakes made with ground almonds are naturally gluten-free but they also have a fabulously moist texture. This one, a variation on the trad orange and almond cake, is no exception. One useful tip – if you happen to have a pressure cooker, you can cook the lemons in ten minutes instead of an hour!

Makes 8–12 slices

2 unwaxed lemons, washed
butter, for greasing
200g ground almonds
1 tsp gluten-free baking
    powder
pinch of salt
5 eggs
200g golden caster sugar

To decorate

1 tbsp caster sugar
50g flaked almonds, lightly
    toasted
a few dried rose petals
    (optional)

Put the lemons in a saucepan and cover them with freshly boiled water. Bring the water back to the boil, cover the pan and simmer until the lemons are soft enough for you to pierce the skin easily with the handle of a wooden spoon. This will probably take at least an hour.

When the lemons are tender, remove them from the water. When they are cool enough to handle, break them open and remove any pips. Put the lemons in a food processor and blitz to form a bright yellow purée. Leave to cool.

Preheat the oven to 170°C/Fan 150°C/Gas 3½. Generously butter a deep 20–21cm cake tin and line it with baking parchment.

Mix the ground almonds with the baking powder and a generous pinch of salt. Beat the eggs in a separate bowl until very well aerated – they should be really foamy. Gradually beat in the sugar, followed by the ground almonds, then fold in the cooled lemon purée.

Pour the mixture into the prepared tin and bake the cake in the preheated oven for 40 minutes until it is well risen and a deep golden brown. Leave to cool in the tin for about 15 minutes, then turn it out on to a wire rack.

When the cake is completely cool, dust it with caster sugar and sprinkle over the almonds – and some rose petals if you fancy.

GRAPEFRUIT POLENTA CAKE

We've made polenta cakes in the past, but we think this one reaches new levels of grown-up sophistication. The grapefruit does bring a wonderful flavour, but you can use the zest from two lemons or oranges or three limes, if you prefer. The touch of Campari in the syrup is a good option if you want to go a bit glam.

**Makes 8–12 slices
or 12 squares**

200g butter, softened, plus
    extra for greasing
300g cornmeal or polenta
2 tsp gluten-free baking
    powder
pinch of salt
175g golden caster sugar
zest of 1½ grapefruits,
    very finely grated
3 eggs

Syrup

125g icing sugar
juice from 2 grapefruits
1 tbsp Campari (optional)

Preheat the oven to 180°C/Fan 160°C/Gas 4. Butter a 23cm round or a 20cm square cake tin, preferably not a loose-bottomed one or the syrup will ooze out, and line it with baking parchment.

Mix the cornmeal or polenta with the baking powder and a generous pinch of salt. Put the butter into a bowl with the sugar and grapefruit zest and beat until very soft and aerated. Add the eggs, one at a time with a couple of tablespoons of the cornmeal or polenta mix, beating well in between each addition, then fold in the remaining cornmeal or polenta. The batter will be quite stiff.

Scrape the mixture into the prepared tin and smooth over the top. Don't worry if it looks a little craggy at this stage, it will even out in the oven. Bake for 35–40 minutes until the top is springy and a rich brown. The cake should also have shrunk away from the sides of the tin.

While the cake is baking, make the syrup. Put the sugar, juice and the Campari, if using, into a small pan and heat until the sugar has dissolved.

Once the cake is done, leave it in the tin and pierce it all over the top with a cocktail stick or skewer. Pour over the syrup while the cake and the syrup are both still hot, making sure you cover the cake as evenly as possible. Leave the cake to cool in the tin, then carefully transfer to a serving plate.

RASPBERRY & MANGO MERINGUES

Meringues are naturally gluten-free, so they're a great option for anyone avoiding gluten, plus they are awesome and delicious. It's well worth making your own – the shop-bought nests are not a patch on home-made and you can be as adventurous as you like with the toppings. We're very happy with this raspberry and mango combo.

Makes 4 large meringue sandwiches or 6 smaller

4 egg whites, at room
   temperature
¼ tsp cream of tartar (optional,
   but advisable)
pinch of salt
220g caster sugar
75g raspberries
1 tbsp icing sugar

Filling

400ml double cream
1 tbsp icing sugar
1 large mango, see method

Preheat your oven to 150°C/Fan 130°C/Gas 2. Take 2 sheets of baking parchment and mark out either 10 or 12cm rounds, well-spaced apart, depending on whether you want to make 8 or 12 meringues. Place the parchment sheets on 2 baking trays.

Put the egg whites in a bowl and sprinkle in the cream of tartar, if using. Whip to the stiff peak stage – at this point the whites will hold their shape and will not budge from the bowl, even if the bowl is turned upside down.

Add a pinch of salt to the sugar. Start adding the sugar to the meringue, a spoonful at time to start with – this will help prevent the meringues from weeping. Once you've added about half the sugar, you can add the rest in larger amounts. You will end up with a well aerated, glossy meringue. Divide the meringue between the baking trays, piling them high on the rounds you have drawn.

Crush the raspberries with the icing sugar to make a very rough purée – push it through a sieve if you prefer, but the seeds do give a good texture. Drizzle a heaped teaspoon of the purée on the top of each meringue, then very carefully and lightly swirl it in. Keep this to an absolute minimum, as you don't want the sauce combining with the meringue or it will turn the mixture an unappetising grey colour!

Bake the meringues in the oven for 1 hour to 1¼ hours until they are dry and crisp. Turn off the oven and leave the meringues for another hour to cool down very slowly. This will help them dry out and keep their shape without cracking. Remove from the oven and leave to cool completely.

For the filling, whip the cream until it is firm, then stir in the icing sugar. Chill until you are ready to serve. Peel and dice the mango, scraping off any pulp from around the stone and adding this to the flesh. Stir the mango through the cream and spread the mixture over the flat side of the meringues, then sandwich them together. Serve immediately.

PEACH UPSIDE-DOWN CAKE

Upside-down cakes make a great option for dessert as well as teatime and this one was inspired by our travels in the Mediterranean. It's great served straight from the oven or warm with some cream or ice cream and it's good cold too. You can use fresh or canned peaches, depending on the time of year.

Makes 8–12 slices

Brown butter
250g unsalted butter, diced

Topping

25g light brown soft sugar
   or demerara sugar
1 tsp ground cinnamon
2 peaches, peeled and sliced
   into segments, or 1 large can
   of peaches (12–14 slices)

Sponge

175g light brown soft sugar
175g gluten-free flour
2 tsp gluten-free baking
   powder
pinch of salt
3 eggs

First make the brown butter. Put the butter in a large frying pan and heat until it has melted and started to boil. Keep boiling, stirring constantly, until the foam subsides and the milk solids sink and turn brown. Pour the butter into a cold bowl or container immediately, making sure you include the brown sediment. Leave to cool until it returns to a solid state. You should end up with 200g of brown butter.

Preheat the oven to 180°C/Fan 160°C/Gas 4. Line a deep 20–21cm round tin with baking parchment. Avoid using a loose-bottomed tin for this cake or the filling will leak out, but if that is all you have, carefully line the tin with foil before adding the baking parchment.

Rub 25g of the brown butter over the base. Mix the 25g of sugar with the cinnamon and sprinkle this over the base too. Arrange the peach slices on top of the butter and sugar.

Put the remaining 175g of brown butter and the 175g of sugar into a bowl and beat until very soft and aerated. In a separate bowl, mix the flour and baking powder together with a pinch of salt.

Add the eggs, one at a time, to the creamed butter and sugar along with a heaped tablespoon of the flour mixture. Beat in between each addition until you have a smooth batter. Fold in the remaining flour mixture.

Spoon the cake batter over the peaches and smooth out the surface. Bake in the oven for 35–40 minutes until the sponge is springy to the touch and a deep golden brown.

Leave the cake to stand for 5–10 minutes. Run a knife around the sides of the tin just to make sure nothing is sticking, then turn the cake out on to a large plate. Remove the baking parchment. Good served hot, warm or cold.

DESS

SERTS

BAKED RICE PUDDING & BLACKBERRY COMPOTE

Si: my mam made proper rice pudding like this, always with some evaporated milk, which helps give it a lovely colour and a beautiful brown skin on top. This has to cook for much longer than the stove-top versions, but it's so good and once it's in the oven you can forget about it – no stirring or risk of sticking. We used to top our pud with a blob of jam but it's great served with this blackberry compote.

Serves 4–6

750ml whole milk
2 bay leaves
1 mace blade
25g butter, diced, plus extra
   for greasing
125g pudding rice
50g light brown soft sugar
410ml can of evaporated milk
rasp of nutmeg

Blackberry compote

300g blackberries
50g caster sugar
pinch of salt
2 bay leaves
squeeze of lemon juice
1 tbsp crème de mûre
   or cassis (optional)

Put the milk in a saucepan with the bay leaves and mace blade. Heat slowly and remove the pan from the heat just before the milk reaches boiling point. Leave to cool down to room temperature.

Preheat the oven to 150°C/Fan 130°C/Gas 2. Generously grease a 1.5-litre ovenproof dish with butter.

Strain the infused milk and put it in the dish with the rice, brown sugar and evaporated milk. Stir to combine, then drop in the cubes of butter and grate some nutmeg on top.

Bake the pudding for about 2½ hours until the rice has swelled and softened and a rich brown skin has developed on top.

To make the blackberry compote, put the blackberries and sugar in a pan with a pinch of salt. Scrunch up the bay leaves a little – they won't break, just bruise – and add them to the pan. Squeeze over the lemon juice and stir, then leave everything to macerate for a few minutes. The sugar will start to dissolve.

Place the pan over a gentle heat and slowly bring the compote to the boil, stirring regularly, until the blackberries have started to break down and the sauce has started to thicken. Add the crème de mûre or cassis, if using. Leave to cool and remove the bay leaves just before serving with the rice pudding.

SPICED PLUM BROWN BETTY

This is a traditional old favourite but our version is full of spice. We like to layer up the topping and filling so you get a nice mix of textures – crispy on top and lovely and soft and chewy in the middle.

Serves 4–6

Topping

100g butter, melted, plus
    extra for greasing
225g brown bread
75g light brown soft sugar
25g demerara sugar
¼ tsp ground cardamom
¼ tsp ground cinnamon
¼ tsp ground cloves
pinch of salt

Filling

50–75g caster sugar
    (depending on how
    sweet the plums are)
¼ tsp ground cardamom
¼ tsp ground cinnamon
¼ tsp ground cloves
1 tbsp cornflour
1kg ripe plums, pitted
    and cut into wedges

Preheat the oven to 180°C/Fan 160°C/Gas 4. Butter a deep ovenproof dish.

First make the topping. Roughly tear or cut up the bread, then put it in a food processor and process into breadcrumbs. Make sure you don't make them too fine – they should be quite a coarse texture for this dish. Add the melted butter, sugars, spices and a pinch of salt. Mix until the breadcrumbs look glossy with butter and are starting to clump together a bit.

For the filling, put the sugar, cardamom, cinnamon, cloves and cornflour in a bowl and mix. Add the plums and stir until they are well coated. They will very quickly start to give out liquid.

Arrange half the plums over the base of your dish. Sprinkle over half the topping mixture, then repeat with the remaining plums and topping.

Place the dish on a baking tray and bake in the oven for 20–25 minutes until the plums are bubbling and the topping has crisped up. Serve with custard, cream or ice cream.

LEMON & PRUNE CHEESECAKE

This is a proper New York style cheesecake, with a layer of soft, alcohol-soaked prunes. It really hits the spot in terms of texture and taste, we reckon. Use fairly plain biscuits, like digestives, rich tea or gingernuts, nothing too buttery. And Marsala or spiced rum are good alternatives to brandy or calvados for the alcohol.

Serves 6–8

Base

50g butter, melted, plus extra for greasing
200g biscuits, such as digestives, blitzed to form crumbs
½ tsp ground cinnamon
pinch of salt

Prunes and syrup

200g soft, pitted prunes (not canned)
75g dark brown soft sugar
200ml brandy, calvados or rum
1 tsp vanilla extract

Filling

450g cream cheese
zest of 2 lemons
1 tsp vanilla extract
150g soured cream
125g light brown soft sugar
35g cornflour or plain flour
pinch of salt
3 eggs, beaten

To serve

double cream

Preheat the oven to 180°C/Fan 160°C/Gas 4. Grease a deep 20cm round loose-bottomed cake tin and line it with baking parchment. Wrap the outside in foil – the cheesecake is cooked in a water bath so it's important to make sure it is watertight.

Mix the biscuit crumbs with the cinnamon and a generous pinch of salt in a bowl, then pour in the melted butter. Mix thoroughly, then press the mixture into the tin. Bake for 15–20 minutes until lightly browned around the edges, then remove and leave to cool. Brush the biscuit base with a small amount of the beaten eggs you're going to use for the filling.

Turn the oven down to 120°C/Fan 100°C/Gas ½.

Put the prunes in a saucepan with the sugar, your choice of spirit and the vanilla extract. Stir gently over a low heat until the sugar has dissolved, then simmer for 5 minutes. Remove from the heat and strain the prunes – they will have taken on some of the flavour of the alcohol and vanilla, and you will be left with a syrup. Roughly chop the prunes – they will quickly form a purée – and spread them over the biscuit base. Set the syrup aside.

To make the filling, put the cream cheese in a bowl with the lemon zest and vanilla extract. Beat until smooth, then stir in the soured cream. In a separate bowl, mix the sugar and cornflour together with a pinch of salt – this helps break up the cornflour, so it combines more evenly with the cream cheese. Stir the sugar mixture into the cream cheese, then beat in the eggs. Pour the mixture over the prunes.

Shake the tin gently and drop it a couple of times on to your work surface to expel any bubbles – you want a dense cheesecake, nothing really airy.

Put the cake tin in a roasting tin and place it in the oven. Pull the oven shelf out slightly and pour freshly boiled water into the roasting tin. It should come halfway up the sides of the cake tin. Bake for about 1¼ to 1½ hours until the cheesecake has set – it should be firm around the sides with a slight wobble in the centre.

Switch off the oven and leave the cheesecake to cool in the residual heat. Once the oven is cool, remove the cheesecake and when it is at room temperature, transfer it to the fridge. Chill for several hours or preferably overnight. This will help the cheesecake develop its dense, fudgy texture. Serve with some of the reserved prune syrup and double cream.

CUSTARD TART

You don't get much more traditional than a good old custard tart and home-made takes it to another level. We love it – and it's much too good for throwing at anybody! No bells and whistles here, just a lovely smooth custard, topped with nutmeg and encased in crisp pastry. There's nothing better.

Serves 6

Pastry
250g plain flour, plus extra
   for dusting
pinch of salt
125g butter, chilled and diced
1 tbsp icing sugar
1 egg yolk
iced water

Filling
500ml double or whipping
   cream
1 vanilla pod, split lengthways
4 eggs
2 egg yolks
60g caster sugar
nutmeg, for grating

First make the pastry. Put the flour in a bowl with a good pinch of salt and add the butter. Rub the butter into the flour until the mixture resembles fine breadcrumbs, then stir in the icing sugar. Mix the egg yolk with a tablespoon of iced water and drizzle it in, then add just enough iced water to bind the pastry together into a dough. Knead gently until the pastry is smooth.

Dust your work surface with flour and roll out the pastry until it's large enough to line an 18cm deep round tin. Lightly dust the pastry with flour (so it doesn't stick), then fold the sides in and sit the pastry in the base of the tin. Unfold the pastry and push it well into the sides of the tin. Leave a little overhang over the edges of the tin to trim later.

Chill the pastry in the fridge for at least an hour. Preheat the oven to 180°C/Fan 160°C/Gas 4. Line the pastry case with baking parchment and baking beans. Bake for 15 minutes, then remove the baking beans and parchment and put the pastry back in the oven for another 5–10 minutes until it is lightly coloured. Reduce the oven temperature to 150°C/Fan 130°C/Gas 2.

To make the filling, put the cream in a saucepan with the vanilla pod. Bring the cream to boiling point and remove the pan from the heat. Put the eggs, egg yolks and sugar into a bowl and whisk until well combined – don't make it too aerated, because you don't want an air-filled custard.

Remove the vanilla pod from the saucepan. Pour the heated cream from a height over the egg mixture, stirring as you do so, then leave so any froth or air bubbles subside.

Place the pastry case (in its tin) on a baking tray. Pour the custard filling through a sieve into the pastry case, then grate over a generous amount of nutmeg so the surface is completely covered.

Bake the tart in the preheated oven for 45–60 minutes until the custard is just set – aim for it to have a slight wobble still in the centre. Remove the tart from the oven and leave it to cool before serving. The custard will continue to firm up as it cools. Enjoy!

GIN KEY LIME PIE

We made this after visiting an amazing artisan gin maker when filming our *Go North* TV series. It's inspired by Dave's mam's favourite northern tipple – gin and lime cordial – and those chocolate lime sweets we loved as kids. This is a really grown-up dessert and the glaze and drizzle on top makes it look like proper patisserie.

Serves 6

Base
200g Oreo cookies
   or digestive biscuits
75g melted butter

Filling
4 egg yolks
zest of 4 limes
150ml lime juice
25ml gin
400g can of condensed milk

Glaze
150ml lime cordial
3 gelatine leaves
25ml gin

Chocolate drizzle (optional)
50g dark chocolate
15g butter
1 tsp golden syrup

Preheat the oven to 180°C/Fan 160°C/Gas 4. To crush the biscuits, either blitz them in a food processor or put them in a bag and have a therapeutic bash with a rolling pin. Stir the butter into the biscuit crumbs. Press the mixture into a 23cm round flan dish or pie tin, being sure to push it up the sides. Bake in the oven for 10–12 minutes, then leave to cool completely.

To make the filling, put the egg yolks into a bowl and add the lime zest. Beat until the egg yolks are well aerated and vastly increased in volume, then whisk in the lime juice and gin, followed by the condensed milk. Stir to make sure everything is completely combined and has made a thick, smooth and still pourable batter.

Pour the filling over the crust, then put it in the fridge to chill for several hours or preferably overnight.

To make the glaze, gently heat the lime cordial in a small pan. Soak the gelatine leaves in cold water until they are soft and pliable, then wring them out and stir them into the warmed cordial until completely dissolved. Stir in the gin. Strain the mixture into a jug and leave to cool completely.

Pour the cooled, still liquid, lime glaze over the pie and then put it back in the fridge to set.

To make the chocolate drizzle, put the ingredients in a bowl and place over a pan of simmering water. Leave to melt until very smooth. Allow the mixture to cool until warm but still liquid, then drizzle lines of chocolate sauce over the set glaze. Make sure the glaze is well-chilled when you do this – you don't want to risk it melting. Keep the tart chilled until ready to serve.

BREAD & BUTTER PUDDING WITH RHUBARB

Rhubarb and a touch of orange works really well in our new version of this classic British pud. Use whatever bread you like, but we think a loaf with some spelt or rye is particularly good – the nutty flavour is nice with rhubarb. Another idea is to use brioche for a softer result. Either way this is fab and if you want to go proper decadent, serve it with some double cream or ice cream.

Serves 4–6

Rhubarb
300g pink rhubarb, cut into
    3cm lengths
50g caster sugar
zest and juice of 1 orange

Custard

2 eggs
1 egg yolk
50g caster sugar
zest of ½ orange
200ml double cream
150ml whole milk
a few drops of orange
    blossom water (optional)

To assemble

butter, for greasing and
    spreading
6 slices of bread
caster sugar, for sprinkling

First cook the rhubarb. Preheat your oven to 200°C/Fan 180°C/Gas 6. Put the rhubarb in a single layer in an ovenproof dish and toss it with the sugar. Sprinkle over the orange zest and pour the orange juice into the dish around the rhubarb. Cover with foil and bake in the oven for about 15 minutes. Take off the foil and continue to cook for another few minutes until the liquid in the dish is syrupy. Remove from the oven, tip everything into a bowl and set it aside to cool down.

To make the custard, put the eggs, egg yolk, sugar and orange zest in a bowl and whisk until well combined. Stir in the cream and milk and the orange blossom water, if using, followed by all but a couple of tablespoons of the syrup from the roasted rhubarb.

Generously butter an ovenproof dish. Butter the slices of bread and cut them in half on the diagonal. Arrange half of them over the base of the dish, butter-side up. Add about two-thirds of the rhubarb, then top with the remaining bread – again, butter-side up.

Pour over the custard mixture, pressing it down to make sure the bread soaks it up. If you have time, leave the pudding to stand for half an hour. Add the remaining rhubarb and drizzle over the remaining syrup. Sprinkle with some caster sugar.

Place the dish on a baking tray and bake in the oven (200°C/Fan 180°C/Gas 6) for 35–40 minutes until the custard has set and has puffed up a bit around the bread. Remove from the oven and leave to stand for a few minutes before serving.

PEACH & BLUEBERRY PIE

There's nothing nicer to follow Sunday lunch than a good fruit pie and this one tastes the business. We had thought about adding a little spice but the flavour of the fruit after macerating is so great, it needs nothing else. Just peachy!

Serves 4–6

Filling
5–6 peaches, peeled and cut
    into wedges
250g blueberries (fresh or frozen)
100g light brown soft sugar
pinch of salt
40g cornflour
squeeze of lemon juice

Pastry

300g plain flour, plus extra
    for dusting
pinch of salt
150g butter, chilled and diced
1 tbsp icing sugar
1 egg yolk
iced water

To finish

1–2 tbsp milk
2 tbsp granulated sugar (optional)

First, macerate the fruit. Put the peaches and blueberries in a bowl. Sprinkle in the sugar with a pinch of salt and mix together, then cover and leave to stand for at least an hour.

For the pastry, put the flour in a bowl with a pinch of salt and add the butter. Rub the butter into the flour until the mixture resembles breadcrumbs, then stir in the icing sugar, egg yolk and enough iced water to bind everything together. Knead briefly until you have a smooth dough.

Lightly flour your work surface. Divide the dough into one-third and two-thirds, then roll out the larger piece to fit a round pie dish. Put the lined pie dish in the fridge to chill. Wrap the remaining pastry and put that in the fridge as well.

Check the fruit – the sugar should have dissolved and the fruit should be sitting in liquid. Strain off the liquid into a saucepan and set the fruit aside. Bring the liquid to the boil, then reduce until it is syrupy. Remove the pan from the heat and leave the syrup to cool.

Whisk the cornflour into the cooled syrup, making sure there are no lumps. Pour this over the fruit, add a squeeze of lemon juice and mix thoroughly.

Put the fruit in the pastry-lined pie dish. Roll out the remaining pastry and use it to cover the entire top of the pie or cut out shapes and arrange them over the top. If completely covering the pie, cut steam holes in the crust. Brush the pastry with the milk and sprinkle with sugar, if using. Put the pie back in the fridge to chill for at least half an hour.

Preheat the oven to 180°C/Fan 160°C/Gas 4. Put a baking tray in the oven to heat up. Place the pie on the baking tray and bake for 35–40 minutes until the pastry is a rich brown and the sauce around the fruit is bubbling.

This is good eaten hot or cold, but we think the flavour works best at room temperature. Serve with cream or ice cream.

PASSION FRUIT SOUFFLÉS

There's no need to be scared of soufflés – they really aren't that tricky, and you can get the crème pat ready and leave it chilling in the fridge, then do the final stage at the last minute. These have a wonderful flavour, perfectly balanced by a scoop of ice cream and some passion fruit pulp. Just the thing for Valentine's night, maybe?

Serves 4

To coat the ramekins
15g butter, softened
2 tsp caster sugar

Soufflés
3–5 passion fruits, depending
  on size
50g caster sugar
25g plain flour
10g cornflour
100g white chocolate, grated
  or finely chopped
100ml whole milk
4 eggs, separated
pinch of salt
½ tsp cream of tartar

To serve
vanilla ice cream
2 passion fruits

You'll need 4 x 100ml ramekins. Rub butter lightly over the insides of the ramekins and sprinkle them with the sugar, patting out any excess. Put them in the fridge to chill.

Scrape out the flesh of the passion fruit into a sieve over a bowl and push it through to extract as much of the juice as possible – you need 75ml. Set the juice aside and discard the seeds.

Now make the crème patissière which will form the base of the soufflés. Mix the sugar, flour, cornflour and white chocolate together in a medium bowl.

Heat the milk in a small saucepan until close to boiling, then pour the milk from a height into the bowl of flour, sugar and chocolate. Whisk vigorously until the chocolate has almost completely melted and you have a smooth sauce. Pour the sauce back into the pan and slowly bring it back to boiling point, whisking constantly until the mixture starts to thicken. At this point add the reserved passion fruit juice and continue whisking until the sauce has thickened to the consistency of a set custard. Remove the pan from the heat and continue to whisk until you are sure the mixture is lump-free, then transfer it to a bowl to cool. When it is at room temperature, transfer it to the fridge and chill for at least half an hour.

Remove the crème patissière from the fridge and beat in the egg yolks. Preheat the oven to 200°C/Fan 180°C/Gas 6.

Put the egg whites in a bowl with a pinch of salt and the cream of tartar and whisk to the dry, stiff peaks stage. Gradually fold the egg whites into the crème patissière, adding just a third of the mixture to start with, then adding the rest. Be very careful at this stage as the mixture should be evenly combined without streaks, but you also need to ensure you don't knock too much air out of it.

Fill the ramekins to the top with the mixture, then smooth across with a palette knife. Run your finger around the inside rim of the ramekin – this will help the soufflés rise evenly.

Put the ramekins in a roasting tin and place it in the oven. Pull the oven shelf out slightly and pour freshly boiled water into the tin to come halfway up the sides of the ramekins. Bake for 12–15 minutes until the soufflés are well risen and golden brown on top. Do not open the oven door until you're sure they are done, as this may cause them to collapse.

Serve the soufflés at the table by breaking into the top and adding a scoop of ice cream and a spoonful of passion fruit flesh.

APPLE TURNOVERS

We've long enjoyed something similar from a certain fast-food restaurant but guess what? Now we can make our own and they're even better! You can use shop-bought puff pastry, but we promise you this rough puff is dead easy and mega good.

Makes 8

Rough puff pastry
225g plain flour, plus extra
    for dusting
pinch of salt
225g butter, chilled and diced
    into 1cm cubes
1 tbsp caster sugar
125ml iced water

Filling

100g golden caster sugar
1 tbsp cornflour
2 tsp ground cinnamon
¼ tsp ground cloves
pinch of salt
50g butter, very soft
juice of ½ lemon
4 or 5 small apples, peeled
    and finely diced (peeled
    weight about 350g)

To finish

3 tbsp milk
2 tbsp golden caster sugar
1 tsp cinnamon

Put the flour in a bowl with a pinch of salt. Add the butter and toss it until all the individual cubes are coated in flour. Rub or mash the cubes of butter so they flatten out – that's all you need to do – don't rub them any smaller. Stir in the sugar, then pour in the water and briefly knead the mixture into a dough, handling it as little as possible. Put the dough in a container and chill in the fridge for half an hour.

Dust your work surface with flour. Roll out the pastry to a rectangle measuring 25 x 35–40cm. The rolled-out pastry will be flecked with pieces of butter and this is exactly what you want.

Cut the rectangle in half, widthways, then fold each piece twice, so it ends up with 4 layers. Chill again, preferably for at least 2 hours, or you can leave the pastry overnight at this stage.

Take the pastry out of the fridge and roll each piece out into a rectangle measuring 28 x 32cm. Dust 2 pieces of baking parchment with flour and carefully place each rectangle on top, then chill until you are ready to use.

Make the filling at the last minute, as the longer you leave it to stand, the more liquid will come out of the apples. Mix the dry ingredients together with a generous pinch of salt. Stir in the butter and lemon juice, followed by the apples.

Cut each piece of pastry into 4 smaller rectangles, each measuring roughly 14 x 16cm.

Place 2 tablespoons of the apple mixture lengthways over half of a pastry rectangle, making sure you leave a 2cm border. Brush the edges with milk, then fold the uncovered half of pastry over the filling and seal. Crimp all the way round the cut edges and place on a baking tray. Continue with the remaining pieces of pastry and filling to make 8 rectangular turnovers.

Chill again for at least an hour. When you are ready to bake, preheat the oven to 200°C/Fan 180°C/Gas 6. Mix the cinnamon and sugar together. Brush each turnover with milk and sprinkle with the cinnamon and sugar. Cut several slits across the turnovers. Bake in the oven for about 30 minutes until the pastry is crisp and golden and the filling is cooked. Wait at least 5 minutes before eating – the filling will be very hot.

These are good hot or cold and keep for several days in an airtight container.

PROFITEROLES

Who doesn't love a profiterole? And home-made ones are really special. Beating the mixture does take a bit of elbow grease, but if you have a stand mixer or electric beaters it's no problem. You can make all the elements in advance, but don't fill the profiteroles too early or they will go soggy.

Serves 4–6

Profiteroles
60g butter
1 tsp caster sugar
75g plain flour
pinch of salt
2 eggs, beaten

Filling

250ml whipping cream
1 tbsp icing sugar
a few drops of vanilla extract
(optional)

White chocolate sauce

150ml double or whipping
cream
100g white chocolate,
broken up

To serve

400g mixture of fresh berries
(raspberries, blueberries,
strawberries, cherries,
redcurrants)

Put the butter and sugar in a saucepan and add 150ml of water. Heat until the butter has melted and the sugar has dissolved, then raise the heat until the mixture is boiling. Reduce the heat to low.

Sift the flour on to a piece of baking parchment and add a good pinch of salt. Pull up the sides of the baking parchment and slide the flour into the butter and sugar mixture. Stir very briskly until you have a thick smooth paste. The paste should pull away from the base of the saucepan and be slightly steaming. Stir for a couple of minutes until the steam subsides and the mixture leaves a slight floury residue on the base of the pan, then remove the pan from the heat and leave to cool for 5 minutes.

Preheat the oven to 200°C/Fan 180°C/Gas 6. Line a baking tray with baking parchment. Dampen the baking parchment – this will create steam which will help crisp up the profiteroles in the oven.

Once the paste has cooled down, gradually beat in the eggs, a couple of tablespoons at a time, until you have a thick, glossy dough. This can be quite hard work, so use a stand mixer or electric beaters, if possible.

Drop 12 tablespoons of the dough on to the baking tray, spacing them out well. Wet a finger and smooth away any rough spots. If you prefer, use a teaspoon and make 24 profiteroles, in which case you will need a couple of baking trays. Bake for about 20 minutes until puffed up and a rich brown.

Remove from the oven. Cut a small slit in the side of each profiterole to allow steam to escape and put them back in the oven for another couple of minutes. Remove and leave to cool, or switch the oven off, leave the door slightly ajar and leave to cool – this will really help crisp them up.

To make the filling, whip the cream and icing sugar together to stiff peaks. Chill until you are ready to fill the profiteroles. Don't do this very far ahead or they may go soggy with the moisture from the cream. Spoon the filling into a piping bag and pipe through the slits you've made in the profiteroles.

To make the chocolate sauce, put the cream and chocolate in a saucepan. Place over a very low heat, stirring regularly, until the chocolate has completely melted, and you have a sauce the consistency of unwhipped double cream. If you want to make this ahead, it will firm up quite considerably as it cools, so you'll need to reheat it very gently before serving.

Serve the filled profiteroles with the warm sauce and a tumble of berries.

ORANGE & RHUBARB MERINGUE PIE

Lemon meringue pie was a great favourite in both our households when we were kids, and we still love it, but it's time to experiment. We're thrilled with this new variation which looks as glorious as it tastes. We've made ours in a tart tin, but if you'd like a more towering layer of meringue you could use a 21–22cm pie dish instead. Spectacular either way.

Serves 4–6

Pastry
200g plain flour, plus extra
    for dusting
100g butter, chilled and diced
pinch of salt
1 egg yolk, beaten,
    for brushing
iced water

Filling
500g rhubarb, cut into
    3cm lengths
100g caster sugar
zest of 3 oranges
250ml freshly squeezed orange
    juice (from about 4 medium
    oranges)
50g cornflour
pinch of salt
4 egg yolks

Meringue
5 egg whites
½ tsp cream of tartar
275g caster sugar

First make the pastry. Put the flour in a bowl with the butter and a generous pinch of salt. Rub in the butter until the mixture resembles fine breadcrumbs, then work in just enough iced water to bring it all together into a dough.

Dust your work surface with flour and roll out the dough to fit a 23–25cm fluted tart tin. Roughly trim the edges a few millimetres above the rim and put the pastry in the fridge to chill for at least an hour.

Preheat the oven to 180°C/Fan 160°C/Gas 4. Line the pastry case with baking parchment and fill it with baking beans. Bake it for 15 minutes, then remove the parchment and beans and brush the pastry liberally with the egg yolk. This is really important as it will help create a seal and prevent a soggy bottom. Put the pastry back in the oven for another 5 minutes.

To prepare the filling, put the rhubarb in a baking tin with half the sugar and the orange zest. Cover the tin with foil and bake for 15 minutes. Remove the foil and put the rhubarb back in the oven for another 5 minutes, just to help the juices reduce and become syrupy. You can bake the rhubarb at the same time as you blind bake the pastry, if you like. Being careful not to break up the rhubarb, place it in a sieve to strain and reserve both flesh and juice.

To make the curd layer, put 75ml of the orange juice in a bowl with the remaining sugar, the cornflour and a pinch of salt. Whisk to a paste. Put the rest of the orange juice in a saucepan and heat it gently. Pour the hot orange juice over the cornflour mixture, stirring constantly, then pour it all back into the pan. Slowly bring the mixture to the boil, stirring or whisking constantly and thoroughly, until it thickens to the consistency of a thick, set custard. Remove from the heat. Beat in the reserved rhubarb syrup and the egg yolks, then set aside to cool. Preheat the oven to 180°C/Fan 160°C/Gas 4 and put a baking tray into the oven to heat up.

To make the meringue, put the egg whites in a bowl with the cream of tartar. Beat to the stiff peaks stage, but before the mixture gets dry (it should still have a little movement), start adding the sugar, a couple of tablespoons at a time. Whisk thoroughly in between each addition. When you have incorporated all the sugar you should have a thick, glossy meringue.

To assemble, arrange the rhubarb over the bottom of the pastry case. Spread over the orange and rhubarb curd. Spoon the meringue on top, using a palette knife to create little curlicues if you like. Place the pie on the heated baking tray and bake for 25–30 minutes until the meringue crust has just set and turned a pale brown. Remove from the oven and serve hot or cold with cream.

SUSSEX POND PUDDING

There's nothing that can beat a classic suet pudding. James Martin made one similar to this for us on *Saturday Kitchen* and it was so good we had to try it for ourselves. When you open the pudding, you're rewarded with a flow of lemony, buttery sauce. Utterly delicious. It's easy to make, although you do have to steam it for up to four hours. If you have a pressure cooker, though, it's done in about an hour and 15 minutes.

Serves 4–6

For the pudding basin
butter, for greasing
demerara sugar, for sprinkling

Pastry
200g self-raising flour, plus
   extra for dusting
pinch of salt
25g butter, chilled and cubed
75g suet
25g light brown soft sugar
4–5 tbsp cold milk, for mixing

Filling

1 large unwaxed lemon
   or 2 limes, washed
100g butter, softened
100g light brown soft sugar
½ tsp ground cinnamon
½ tsp mixed spice (optional)

Generously butter a 750ml–1 litre pudding basin with butter, then sprinkle it with a couple of tablespoons of demerara sugar.

For the suet pastry, put the flour in a bowl with a generous pinch of salt and add the butter and suet. Rub them in until the mixture resembles breadcrumbs, then stir in the sugar and just enough of the milk to form a stiff dough, making sure it isn't sticky.

Dust your work surface with flour. Take about three-quarters of the dough and roll it into a round to fit the basin. Use it to line the basin, making sure the dough is pushed right into the corners with a little overlap over the edges.

Cut deep slits all over the lemon or limes. Mix the butter and sugar together with the cinnamon and mixed spice, if using. Put half this mixture in the bottom of the lined basin, then place the lemon or limes on top. Put the rest of the butter and sugar mixture on top of the fruit.

Roll out the remaining pastry into a round to make a lid for the pudding. Place this on top of the filling and crimp the edges to seal them.

If your pudding basin has a lid, place this on top. Alternatively, butter a piece of foil or baking parchment and fold a pleat into it. Secure it over the basin with string or a couple of elastic bands.

Place the basin in a steamer or on top of a folded napkin in a large saucepan. Pour freshly boiled water into the base of the steamer or into the saucepan so it comes halfway up the basin. Steam for 3½ to 4 hours, making sure you keep the water level topped up.

Check to see if the pudding is done – the crust should be a rich golden brown. Very carefully run a palette knife around the rim to loosen the pudding, then turn it out on to a plate. Serve with cream.

LEMON & BLUEBERRY PAVLOVA

A fabulous pavlova says celebration to us and this version with plenty of tangy citrus is no exception. It's a great addition to any feast – what's not to love?

Serves 6

Meringue base
6 large egg whites
300g caster sugar
1 tsp cornflour
1 tsp white wine vinegar

Syrup
100g granulated sugar
juice and pared zest of 2 lemons
2 tbsp yuzu, grapefruit or mandarin juice (optional, add more lemon juice if you prefer)
1 tbsp tequila (optional)

To assemble
300ml double or whipping cream
1 tbsp icing sugar
300g blueberries

Preheat the oven to 160°C/Fan 140°C/Gas 3. Line a baking sheet with baking parchment and draw a 23cm round on the baking parchment for guidance for the meringue base.

Whisk the egg whites until they form soft peaks, then gradually add the sugar, a tablespoon at a time to start with. Whisk vigorously in between each addition, until the meringue is stiff and glossy. Mix the cornflour and vinegar together and whisk into the meringue.

Pile the meringue on to the circle on your baking parchment, making sure you leave a dip in the middle and build the sides up a bit. Put the meringue in the oven and right away turn the temperature down to 150°C/Fan 130°C/Gas 2. Bake for an hour, then turn off the heat, leave the oven door ajar and allow the pavlova to cool in the oven.

To make the syrup, put the sugar and the lemon juice and zest into a small saucepan. Slowly heat, stirring constantly, until the sugar has dissolved, then bring to the boil. Turn down to a simmer and cook until the syrup reaches the thread stage – this will take about 10 minutes and the mixture should reach a temperature of 112°C. To check, drizzle a small amount of the syrup into a glass of cold water – it it's ready, it will form fine threads, not dissolve.

Add the extra citrus juice and bring the syrup back to the same temperature, then remove the pan from the heat. Add the tequila, if using, and leave to cool down – the syrup should thicken as it cools. Strain it before using.

Whip the cream with the icing sugar until thick but not too stiff. Put the cream in the centre of the meringue and drizzle over half the syrup. Give the cream a couple of quick stirs, then add a little more syrup. Pile on the blueberries and drizzle over the remaining syrup.

CAN
&P
FO

APÉS

ETITS

OURS

MUSHROOM VOL-AU-VENTS

Don't dismiss vol-au-vents as the preserve of an Alan Ayckbourn play. For us, they've never gone out of fashion and they're just the thing to serve with a few drinks at Christmas or any other time. You can prepare the pastry cases in advance, then just reheat and fill when you're ready to serve them. And yes, vol-au-vents are often round, but we like these square ones – less wastage of the pastry and any trimmings are a good shape for cheese straws!

Makes 30

Pastry cases
flour, for dusting
500g block of puff pastry
1 egg, beaten

Filling

1 tbsp olive oil
25g butter
1 shallot, very finely chopped
1 thyme sprig
500g small mushrooms, finely
    sliced
2 garlic cloves, crushed
    or grated
zest of ½ lemon
15g plain flour
2 tbsp Marsala
150ml whole milk
50ml double cream
leaves from 2 large tarragon
    sprigs, finely chopped
squeeze of lemon (optional)
drizzle of truffle oil (optional)
cayenne, for sprinkling
salt and black pepper

First make the pastry cases. Preheat the oven to 180°C/Fan 160°C/Gas 4. Line 2 baking trays with baking parchment.

Lightly dust your work surface with flour and roll out the pastry into a rectangle measuring about 30 x 25cm. Trim so that the edges are straight, then cut it into 30 squares. Score a border around each square with a knife, making sure you don't cut all the way through the pastry.

Place the squares on the baking trays, then brush them with the beaten egg. Bake for 15–18 minutes until well puffed up and golden brown, then remove from the oven. When the pastry is cool enough to handle, cut through the score lines and push the centre of each case down to make a rectangular, steep-sided well. Set aside.

For the filling, heat the oil and butter in a large frying pan. Add the shallot and thyme and sauté for several minutes until the shallot is soft and translucent. Turn up the heat, add the mushrooms and fry them until they have reduced in size and any liquid has evaporated – they should look glossy, but not wet. Add the garlic and lemon zest and sauté for another couple of minutes.

Stir in the flour – this will create a paste around the mushrooms – then add the Marsala. Stir – the mixture will get very thick – then gradually work in all the milk, followed by the cream. Stir in half the tarragon and season with salt and pepper. Taste and add a squeeze of lemon juice if you feel the filling needs it.

If you want to serve the vol-au-vents warm (and they are better this way), put the pastry in a warm oven for 5 minutes to heat through, then spoon the filling into the cavities. Drizzle over a little truffle oil, if using, then garnish with the rest of the chopped tarragon and pinches of cayenne. Serve immediately.

GOUGÈRES

These melting little mouthfuls of savoury choux pastry are totally epic. You may think 48 is a lot to make but believe us, they will disappear as soon as you get them out of the oven and people will ask for more. You can use any hard cheese and this is a good way of finishing up any odds and ends in the fridge. These are great just as they are, but you can also fill your gougères with cream cheese or pâté.

Makes 48

85g unsalted butter
1 tsp Marmite or a pinch of salt
150g plain flour, well sieved
1 tsp mustard powder
½ tsp dried thyme
4 eggs
75g hard cheese, such as
   Comté, Cheddar or Gruyère,
   very finely grated
25g Parmesan, very finely grated

To finish

10g Gruyère, very finely grated
10g Parmesan, very finely grated

Line 2 baking trays with baking parchment. Fix a 1–1.5cm round nozzle on a piping bag.

Put the butter, the Marmite or salt and 250ml of water into a saucepan. Bring to the boil and stir until the butter has melted.

Sift the flour on to a piece of baking parchment with the mustard and add the thyme. Pull up the sides of the parchment and slide the flour all at once into the melted butter mixture. Whisk until the batter is smooth – it will start to steam but continue to cook for another couple of minutes, until the mixture comes away from the sides and base of the pan. It will also leave a very fine layer on the base of the pan. Remove the pan from the heat and leave to cool for 5 minutes. Preheat the oven to 200°C/Fan 180°C/Gas 6.

Beat in the eggs one at a time, whisking thoroughly after each addition. You can use a stand mixer for this if you prefer – it does require some elbow grease. When all the eggs have been incorporated, stir in both cheeses.

Spoon about half of the mixture into the piping bag and pipe 4cm rounds on to the baking trays, spacing them evenly apart. If you prefer, you can use a teaspoon instead of a piping bag. Then wet a finger and smooth out any rough tips on the rounds.

Mix the 10g of Gruyère and 10g of Parmesan together and sprinkle half of the mixture over the rounds. Bake the gougères in the oven for 10 minutes, then turn the oven down to 180°C/Fan 160°C/Gas 4 and cook for another 10–15 minutes, until they are well puffed up and dry in the centre.

Check to see if the gougères are done – they should sound hollow when tapped. Remove them from the oven and cut a small slit in the side of each one to let steam escape. Put them back in the oven for a further 5 minutes to help the insides dry out. Repeat with the remaining dough and cheese.

These are best eaten while still warm, but they can be stored in an airtight container and reheated in the oven. Just bake for another 5 minutes at 180°C/Fan 160°C/Gas 4.

PARMESAN CUSTARD TARTS

Mmm – seriously nice and a real treat for those who don't have a sweet tooth. They're perfect for a buffet table or to hand round as canapés with drinks when you're going super smart! We've made the pastry cases a touch thicker than usual so that they are robust enough to hold the filling and don't crumble away in your hand.

Makes 12

Preheat the oven to 180°C/Fan 160°C/Gas 4.

Pastry
300g plain flour
½ tsp salt
75g butter, chilled and
   diced
75g lard, chilled and diced
50g Parmesan, finely grated
1 egg yolk
iced water

Custard filling
100ml single cream
300ml double cream
1 garlic clove, cut in half
1 thyme sprig
50g Parmesan, finely grated
75g Gruyère or similar hard
   cheese, finely grated
4 egg yolks
pinch of cayenne
salt and white pepper

First make the pastry. Put the flour into a large bowl and add the salt. Add the butter and lard and rub it into the flour until the mixture resembles fine breadcrumbs. Stir in the Parmesan and add the egg yolk, then mix, adding just enough iced water to make a firm dough. Make sure the dough isn't too dry – it will need to have some pliability.

Roll out the pastry and cut out 12 rounds, each measuring 10–12cm. Use the rounds to line a 12-hole muffin tin, then place them in the fridge to chill for at least half an hour.

Line each pastry case with a piece of baking parchment and some baking beans. Bake for 10–15 minutes until the pastry has set, then remove the beans and parchment and bake for a further 5 minutes. Remove from the oven and leave to cool.

To make the custard filling, put the creams into a saucepan with the garlic and thyme, and heat very gently until the mixture is at blood temperature. Leave to infuse for 10 minutes. Reserve a tablespoon of the Parmesan for sprinkling, then add the rest of the cheeses to the cream. Season with salt and a very little sprinkle of white pepper, then stir over a very low heat until the cheese has melted. Allow to cool completely, then beat in the eggs. Strain the mixture through a sieve into a jug.

Preheat the oven to 160°C/Fan 140°C/Gas 3. Pour the cooled mixture into the pastry cases. Sprinkle over the reserved Parmesan and a little cayenne, then bake the tarts in the oven for about 20 minutes until the custards are just set – they should still have a slight wobble in the middle. These are best served at room temperature.

VINDALOO SAUSAGE ROLLS

The sausage roll but not as you know it – these are sausage rolls with attitude. The spicy paste makes these into something fabulously spicy and intensely savoury that will really impress and delight your friends.

Makes 24

500g sausage meat
a few coriander sprigs,
    finely chopped
1 x 320g pack of
    ready-rolled puff pastry
pinch of turmeric
1 egg, beaten
1 tsp nigella seeds

Vindaloo paste

1 onion (see method)
15g root ginger, peeled and
    roughly chopped
3 garlic cloves, roughly chopped
3–4 red chillies, deseeded and
    roughly chopped
1 tbsp olive oil
1 tsp ground cumin
1 tsp turmeric
1 tsp ground coriander
1 tsp medium chilli powder
½ tsp ground fenugreek
½ tsp ground cinnamon
2 tbsp tomato purée
1 tbsp malt vinegar
2 tsp jaggery or light brown
    soft sugar
salt

First make the vindaloo paste. Cut the onion in half. Roughly chop half of it, then put it in a food processor with the ginger, garlic and chillies and purée to form a smooth paste, adding a little water if necessary.

Finely chop the remaining onion half. Heat the olive oil in a frying pan, add the chopped onion and fry until translucent. Add the spices and stir for another couple of minutes, then add the onion paste and the tomato purée. Stir for a few minutes – the aim is to cook the mixture a little, so it reduces until it's thick and starting to separate. Add the malt vinegar and sugar. Season with plenty of salt and cook for another couple of minutes or so to dissolve the sugar. Remove from the heat and leave to cool.

Break up the sausage meat and mix in the coriander. Preheat the oven to 180°C/Fan 160°C/Gas 4.

Unroll the puff pastry and cut it in half, lengthways. Thickly spread the vindaloo paste down the centre of each piece of puff pastry. Leave a centimetre of border along each long side, but make sure you go right to the edge of the short sides.

Divide the sausage meat into 2 pieces and shape them into logs the same length as the pastry. Place each log along one of the long edges on each piece of pastry.

Whisk the turmeric into the beaten egg. Brush the exposed edge of the pastry with egg, then roll up and make sure the edges are sealed. Cut each roll into 12 pieces.

Place the sausage rolls on a couple of baking sheets, then brush with the remaining egg and sprinkle with the nigella seeds. Bake for about 25 minutes until the pastry is crisp and the filling is cooked through. Good hot or cold.

RUM BALLS

These make really cute little petits fours and are a great way of using up cake that's past its best or, as we did, using trimmings from making a Battenberg (see page 68). This is a very good-tempered recipe, and you can use whatever fruit juice, alcohol and jam works best with your cake. It's easily doubled too, if you want lots.

Makes 20

250g stale or leftover cake
100ml freshly squeezed orange juice or other fruit juice
1 tbsp jam
20g cocoa powder
1 tbsp rum or similar

To fill (optional)

100g marzipan (shop-bought or see p. 267) or 20 cherries in syrup, drained and blotted

To roll

2 tbsp cocoa powder or desiccated coconut or ground almonds

Put the cake in a bowl with the fruit juice, jam, cocoa powder and rum. Beat together until you have a thick paste – it's easiest to do this in a food processor or in a stand mixer with the paddle attachment if you have one.

Leave the mixture to chill in the fridge for half an hour to firm up. If using the marzipan, roll it into 20 small balls. Divide the cake mixture into 20 portions and roll into spheres, or, if including a filling, mould the mixture around the marzipan or cherries.

Roll the balls in the cocoa powder, coconut or ground almonds, then drop them into petits fours cases. Chill until ready to serve.

GOAT'S CHEESE FILO CIGARS

As you'll see, we've gone with a bit of a Caribbean vibe here and added some scotch bonnet to pep up our cigars. You could use other chillies if you prefer. One of the great things about these is you can get them ready in advance, then pop them in the oven at the last minute, so they're just the thing for entertaining. They're easy to make but just be sure to include nice dry breadcrumbs to absorb excess moisture from the cheese, don't wrap the cigars too tightly, and be sure not to skimp on the chilling. You can also double or triple this recipe if you're catering for a crowd.

Makes 16

Filling
125g soft goat's cheese
25g dry breadcrumbs
2 spring onions, finely chopped
zest of 1 lime
½–1 scotch bonnet, deseeded
  and finely chopped
leaves from 1 thyme sprig
¼ tsp ground allspice
salt and black pepper

Pastry
8 large filo pastry sheets,
  cut into quarters
100ml butter, melted

Topping
2 tbsp runny honey
½ tsp ground allspice
¼ tsp ground cinnamon

First make the filling. Put all the ingredients in a bowl and add plenty of salt and pepper. Mix thoroughly and then leave the filling to chill in the fridge until you are ready to use it, preferably for at least half an hour.

When you are ready to make the cigars, take a piece of filo and brush it lightly with butter. Place another piece of filo on top. Take a heaped teaspoon of the filling (about 10g) and shape it into a log to fit along the lower half of the filo, leaving 2cm borders at the bottom, left and right. Roll the exposed bottom edge of filo over the filling, then fold in the side edges. Brush the folded edges with more butter then roll up. Make sure you don't roll it too tightly as this can cause the cigars to burst in the oven.

Brush the seam and the top with butter and place the cigar on a lined baking tray. Repeat with the remaining pastry and filling – you should end up with 16 cigars.

Chill the cigars in the fridge for at least another 30 minutes. You can make them in advance to this point and leave them in the fridge for a day or so, or open freeze them before transferring them to a container or freezer bag.

When you are ready to bake, preheat the oven to 200°C/Fan 180°C/Gas 6. Bake the cigars for about 10 minutes from chilled or 15 minutes from frozen, until golden brown.

Warm the honey to melt it, then use it to brush the top of the still-hot cigars. Mix the ground allspice and cinnamon with a pinch of salt and sprinkle this over the cigars. Serve warm.

MINI FAIRY CAKES

Decorative and dainty, bite-sized fairy cakes are perfect for a children's party or any party, really. You can flavour these with any kind of citrus – lime is good – and you can top them with sherbert or popping candy instead of the lemon zest, if you like. The citric acid is optional but it does add a nice extra hit to the flavour. Be sure to use the food-grade kind, though, not the stuff sold for cleaning!

Makes 24

100g butter, softened,
   plus extra for greasing
100g golden caster sugar
grated zest of 1 lemon
pinch of salt
2 eggs
100g self-raising flour

Icing

100g icing sugar
juice of up to 1 lemon

To decorate

pared zest of 1 lemon,
   cut into thin strips
2 tbsp caster sugar
¼ tsp food-grade citric acid
   (optional)

Preheat the oven to 180°C/Fan 160°C/Gas 4. Either butter a 24-hole mini fairy cake tin or line the holes with mini paper cases.

Put the butter, sugar and lemon zest in a bowl with a pinch of salt. Beat for a couple of minutes until soft and increased a little in volume. Add one of the eggs with half the flour and mix to combine, then fold in the remaining egg and the rest of the flour.

Spoon the mixture into the prepared tin and bake for about 15 minutes until the cakes are cooked through, golden brown and springy to touch. Remove them from the oven and leave to cool in the tin.

To make the icing, sieve the icing sugar to make sure there are no lumps, then gradually whisk in just enough lemon juice to make a thick glaze. Always make it thicker than you think it needs to be, as it will become very runny, very quickly. Spoon the icing over the cakes and leave to set.

To make the lemon garnish, put the strips of lemon zest on a baking tray and leave them in oven while it cools down to dry out for at least an hour. Then put them in a food processor and blitz with the caster sugar and the citric acid, if using. Sprinkle this over the cakes just before serving.

MINI FLORENTINES

We first made florentines in a Christmas special we filmed some years ago. We thought it was time for another look and this is the result – indulgent, fabulous and just enough chew. A box of these would make a lovely little gift at Christmas. Our recipe makes 48 bite-sized florentines that are ideal for parties, but you could make 24 larger ones if you prefer.

Makes 24–48

30g butter
60g demerara sugar
zest of 1 lime
2 tbsp double cream
50g glacé cherries, chopped
50g dates or figs, finely chopped
50g flaked almonds
50g pistachios or pecans, chopped
15g plain flour
½ tsp ground cinnamon
125g dark chocolate, broken up
salt

Preheat the oven to 200°C/Fan 180°C/Gas 6. You will need a 24-hole silicone baking tray or non-stick tin or a couple of baking trays lined with some baking parchment.

Put the butter, sugar and lime zest in a small saucepan with a generous pinch of salt. Melt together over a low heat, stirring every so often. When the sugar has dissolved, remove the pan from the heat and whisk in the cream to make a smooth caramel.

Put the fruit, nuts, flour and cinnamon in a bowl with another pinch of salt. Pour the caramel over them and mix thoroughly.

Spoon scant teaspoons of the mixture into your 24-hole tray or tin or on to lined baking trays. Keep them well spaced apart if using baking trays. The mixture will make up to 48 small florentines, so you may have to cook them in a couple of batches.

Bake in the oven for 12–14 minutes until lightly browned. The caramel will have set around the fruit and nuts but will still be pliable. If you have made these on a baking tray, they will probably have spread into uneven shapes. If this is the case, take a knife or spoon and gently push them back into shape while the caramel is still soft. Leave the florentines to cool until hard.

Put the chocolate in a heatproof bowl and place over a saucepan of simmering water until melted. Turn the florentines over to expose their smooth undersides. Spoon the chocolate over them and use a fork to make curved lines over the chocolate if you want to be traditional.

Leave the florentines to cool and harden on a wire rack, then transfer them to an airtight tin.

CHOCOLATE FRIDGE CAKE

There's room in everyone's life for a fridge cake – the favourite no-bake bake! We've come up with a slightly fancier version than usual, with the addition of the ginger wine and stem ginger, but we still use the familiar fridge cake skills of bashing biscuits and melting chocolate. Feel free to adapt the ingredients as you like.

Makes 12 fingers or 24 small squares

150g raisins
100ml ginger wine or 100ml diluted ginger cordial
125g butter
150g dark chocolate, broken up
150g milk chocolate, broken up
50g golden syrup
3 pieces of stem ginger, finely diced
pinch of salt
200g shortbread or gingernut biscuits, broken or cut up
50g almonds, roughly chopped
50g glacé cherries, halved

Line a 20 x 20cm square tin with baking parchment.

Put the raisins in a small saucepan and pour over the ginger wine or cordial. Add just enough water to cover the raisins, if necessary, then bring to the boil. Simmer for a couple of minutes, then remove the pan from the heat and set aside to cool.

Put the butter, dark and milk chocolate, golden syrup and stem ginger into a heatproof bowl. Add a good pinch of salt, then place the bowl over a saucepan of gently simmering water until the butter and chocolate have melted. Whisk to make sure everything is completely combined.

Strain the raisins if any liquid remains, then add to them to the chocolate mix, along with the biscuits, almonds and glacé cherries. Mix thoroughly. Press the mixture into the lined tin, making it as smooth on top as possible.

Leave to cool, then transfer to the fridge to chill and set. When the cake is solid, cut it into fingers or small squares. Store in the fridge.

FRIANDS

Get your friends round for some friands! Small and perfectly formed, these are the business. We've tried a couple of different flavour combos and we like to use almonds or pistachios and some fig jam, but obviously add whatever jam is your favourite.

Makes 24

100g butter, melted and left to cool, plus extra for greasing
85g ground almonds or pistachios
25g plain flour
125g icing sugar, plus extra for dusting
pinch of salt
3 egg whites
zest of 1 lemon
jam
25g almond or pistachio nibs

Preheat the oven to 200°C/Fan 180°C/Gas 6. Lightly butter the holes in a 24-hole fairy cake tin or silicone tray.

Put the nuts, plain flour and icing sugar into a bowl with a pinch of salt and whisk to combine. In a separate bowl, whisk the egg whites until they are very foamy but still quite wet – not quite at the soft peak stage but almost. Fold the egg whites into the dry ingredients, then whisk in the lemon zest and the melted butter.

Spoon the mixture into the prepared tin – there should be enough mixture for a scant dessertspoonful per hole. Add half a teaspoon of jam to each friand and gently swirl it into the batter so it isn't completely exposed. Sprinkle with the almond or pistachio nibs.

Bake in the preheated oven for about 15 minutes until the friands are lightly golden. Leave to cool, then dust with icing sugar before serving.

MINCEMEAT & MARZIPAN TWISTS

A fun twist on the traditional mince pies to serve at a Christmas party. Make sure you chill the pastry well before making the twists, but even if you have to do a bit of patching here and there, they'll still taste great.

Makes about 28

1 x 320g pack of ready-rolled
   puff pastry
flour, for dusting
4 heaped tbsp mincemeat
   (shop-bought or see p.268)
200g marzipan (shop-bought
   or see p.267), chilled
½ tsp ground cinnamon
1 egg, beaten, for brushing

Topping

50g icing sugar
1 tsp ground cinnamon
   (optional)

Unroll the puff pastry and carefully cut it in half. Dust a piece of baking parchment with flour and put a piece of pastry on it. Spread it with the mincemeat, spreading it as evenly as possible, right to the edges.

Coarsely grate the marzipan over the mincemeat. It might look like a lot because it is grated, but it will press down considerably. Sprinkle over the cinnamon. Carefully place the other piece of puff pastry over the top. Dust with flour, then very gently but firmly, roll over it with a rolling pin. Put it in the fridge for at least half an hour so the pastry firms up.

Preheat the oven to 180°C/Fan 160°C/Gas 4. Line 2 baking trays with baking parchment.

Remove the pastry from the fridge. Cut it in half lengthways – the easiest way to do this is with a pizza wheel – then cut it into strips, 1–1.5cm thick. You should end up with around 28 pieces. Twist each strip by holding both ends and turning your hands in opposite directions. Arrange them on the baking trays and brush with beaten egg.

Bake in the preheated oven for 20–25 minutes until golden brown and crisp. Remove from the oven and leave to cool.

Mix the icing sugar and cinnamon, if using, and dust the twists liberally. They will keep for a few days in an airtight container. If you want to reheat them before serving, don't dust with the icing sugar until after reheating.

ASICS
SIDES

VEGETABLE STOCK

It can be hard to make veg stock tasty, but we think we've succeeded. This is a good stock for use in gravies, such as the sausage gravy on page 46. Great for soups too.

Makes about 1.5 litres

1 tsp olive oil
2 large onions, roughly chopped
3 large carrots, chopped
200g squash or pumpkin, unpeeled, diced
4 celery sticks, sliced
2 leeks, sliced
100ml white wine or vermouth
1 large thyme sprig
1 large parsley sprig
1 bay leaf
a few black peppercorns

Heat the olive oil in a large saucepan. Add all the vegetables and fry them over a high heat, stirring regularly, until they start to brown and caramelise around the edges. This will take at least 10 minutes. Add the white wine or vermouth and boil until it has evaporated away.

Cover the vegetables with 2 litres of water and add the herbs and black peppercorns. Bring to the boil, then turn the heat down to a gentle simmer. Cook the stock, uncovered, for about an hour, stirring every so often.

Check the stock – the colour should have some depth to it. Strain it through a colander or a sieve lined with muslin or kitchen paper into a bowl. Store it in the fridge for up to a week or you can freeze it.

CHICKEN STOCK

If you want to make a larger amount of stock, save up your chicken carcasses in the freezer or add more chicken wings for extra flavour.

Put the chicken bones and the wings, if using, into a saucepan, just large enough for all the chicken to fit quite snugly. Cover with cold water and bring to the boil, then skim off any foam that collects. Add the remaining ingredients and turn the heat down to a very low simmer. Partially cover the saucepan with a lid.

Leave the stock to simmer for about 3 hours, then remove the pan from the heat. Strain the stock through a colander or a sieve lined with muslin or kitchen paper into a bowl.

The stock can be used right away, although it's best to skim off most of the fat that will collect on the top. If you don't need the stock immediately, leave it to cool. The fat will set on top and will be much easier to remove.

You can keep the stock in the fridge for up to 5 days or you can freeze it.

Makes about 1 litre

at least 1 chicken carcass, pulled apart
4 chicken wings (optional)
1 onion, unpeeled, cut into quarters
1 large carrot, cut into large chunks
2 celery sticks, roughly chopped
1 leek, roughly chopped
1 tsp black peppercorns
3 bay leaves
1 large parsley sprig
1 small thyme sprig
a few garlic cloves, unpeeled (optional)

BEEF STOCK

Good stock is an important building block for any pie. This is a really delicious stock that will add flavour and depth to any meat dish. It's great to have in the freezer and perfect for the steak bakes on page 44. Don't chuck out the piece of meat – it's good in sandwiches or can be sliced, fried and added to salads.

Makes about 2 litres

1.5.kg beef bones, including
    marrow bones if possible,
    cut into small lengths
500g piece of beef shin or
    any cheap, fairly lean cut
2 onions, unpeeled, roughly
    chopped
1 leek, roughly chopped
2 celery sticks, roughly chopped
2 carrots, roughly chopped
2 tomatoes
½ tsp black peppercorns
bouquet garni made up of large
    sprigs of thyme and parsley
    and 2 bay leaves

Put the beef bones and meat into a large saucepan and cover them with cold water – at least 3–3.5 litres. Bring the water to the boil and when a starchy, mushroom-grey foam appears, start skimming. Keep on skimming as the foam turns white and continue until it has almost stopped developing.

Add the vegetables, peppercorns and bouquet garni, turn down the heat until the stock is simmering very gently, then partially cover the pan with a lid. Leave to simmer for 3–4 hours.

Line a sieve or colander with 2 layers of muslin or kitchen paper and place it over a large bowl. Ladle the stock into the sieve or colander to strain it. Remove the meat and set it aside, then discard everything else. Pour the strained stock into a large container and leave it to cool. The fat should solidify on top of the stock and will be very easy to remove. You can keep the stock in the fridge for 2 or 3 days or you can freeze it.

BACON JAM

We love bacon and this savoury delight is great with the cornbread muffins on page 84. Try it on some hot buttered toast too. You might be surprised to see coffee in the ingredients, but it really does lift the flavour. Ordinary instant doesn't cut it, but coffee made with instant espresso powder works fine.

Put the bacon in a large saucepan and fry it over a medium heat until it's starting to crisp up and brown. Add the onion and continue to cook until it has softened and is slightly caramelised. Add the garlic and thyme and cook for another minute or so.

Add the vinegar, sugar, maple syrup, coffee and alcohol to the saucepan. Cook over a low heat, stirring constantly to dissolve the sugar. Stir in the chipotle paste or chilli powder, then leave to simmer gently for about an hour, until the mixture is thick and syrupy.

Using a stick blender, if you have one, or an ordinary jug blender, blend the mixture quite roughly – you want to keep plenty of texture in there, so a couple of blasts should be enough. Stir again to mix.

Transfer the jam to a clean, sterilised jar and store it in the fridge. It will keep for up to a month.

Makes 1 large jar

500g smoked streaky bacon, finely diced
2 medium onions, very finely chopped
2 garlic cloves, finely chopped
1 thyme sprig, left whole
75ml cider vinegar
75g light brown soft sugar
50ml maple syrup
100ml strong espresso coffee
100ml bourbon, whisky or brandy
1 tbsp chipotle paste or 1 tsp chilli powder

SHORTCRUST PASTRY

We've included lots of pastry variations throughout this book to go with particular recipes, but we thought you might like a basic all-purpose shortcrust as well. The key to making good pastry is to keep it cool, so using a food processor or a stand mixer instead of rubbing the fat in with your fingertips, can help. In very hot weather, grating in butter straight from the freezer is a good tip. Using half butter and half lard makes a much shorter, flakier pastry. We like to include an egg in pastry as it makes a slightly more elastic, less crumbly dough that is easier to work with.

Makes about 500g

300g plain flour, plus extra
   for dusting
75g butter, chilled and diced
75g lard, chilled and diced
   (or another 75g butter)
pinch of salt
1 egg, beaten (optional)
iced water

Put the flour, butter and lard, if using, in a bowl and add a generous pinch of salt. Rub the fat into the flour, using just your fingertips to keep it as cool as possible, until the mixture resembles fine breadcrumbs. Give the bowl a gentle shake – this will help any larger lumps move to the top which you can then rub until finer, as necessary.

If using the egg, whisk it with a tablespoon of iced water before adding it to the bowl – mixing with the water helps the egg yolk disperse more evenly. Add just enough iced water to the bowl to form a dough.

Knead the dough very gently until smooth, then turn it out on to a floured work surface. If you're using it to line a tart tin or pie dish, roll it out, line the tin or dish, then chill. Alternatively, if the dough is too soft to manage, put it in a container in the fridge and chill it for half an hour first. If you're making things like pasties, you'll need to chill the pastry before rolling.

If you need to roll out pastry that is hard from being chilled, remove it from the fridge at least half an hour before you want to use it and cover it with a damp tea towel. This will help soften it up a bit and stop it from feeling too dry or crumbly around the edges. Use the pastry as needed.

VARIATIONS

Sweet pastry: Add 1 tablespoon of icing sugar. You can also flavour a sweetened dough with citrus zest – add the zest of 1 lemon or orange or 2 limes with the flour.

A more robust pastry: Use suet in place of the 75g of lard or extra butter.

Nutty pastry: Substitute ground almonds or hazelnuts for up to half the flour.

PIZZA DOUGH

We thought you might like a recipe for pizza dough to play around with. When you're ready to cook your pizzas, preheat the oven to its highest temperature and put a couple of upturned baking trays in the oven to heat up. Top with your chosen topping, whether a simple tomato sauce and mozzarella or something more fancy. Dust the baking trays with a little flour and place the pizzas on the trays. Cook for 6–7 minutes until lightly crisped around the edges and dappled brown.

Enough for 4 medium or 6 mini pizzas

250g strong white bread flour, plus extra for dusting
1 tsp fast-acting yeast
1 tsp salt
150ml tepid water
1 tbsp olive oil

Mix the flour and yeast together in a large bowl, then add the salt. Make a well in the centre and gradually work in the water and olive oil, until the mixture comes together as a dough.

Turn the dough out on to a floured work surface and knead until it is smooth and springy. This will take about 10 minutes or 5 minutes in a stand mixer with a dough hook.

Put the dough in a clean, lightly oiled bowl and cover it with a damp tea towel. Leave it somewhere warm for an hour or so until doubled in size.

Turn the dough out again and knock it back, then divide it into 4 or 6 pieces. Shape them into balls, then roll out each piece thinly, stretching it out until it stops springing back. Finish as desired.

BREAD ROLLS

This is the same dough recipe as for our basic bread on page 142, but we thought you might like to know how to bake rolls as well. Nothing like a freshly baked roll to make a simple meal special.

Put the flour in a large bowl and mix in the yeast. Add the salt and the sugar, honey or malt extract. Slowly work in the tepid water until you have a fairly sticky dough. If you are using wholemeal or granary flour, you will probably need more water – up to 350ml. Just make sure that the dough is quite soft and not at all floury looking.

Cover the bowl with a damp tea towel and leave the dough to stand for half an hour. The gluten will start to react during this time, making kneading easier. Turn the dough out on to a work surface dusted with flour and knead until it is smooth and elastic. A good way of telling whether the dough is ready is to apply the windowpane test – very gently pull the dough apart and it should stretch to form a very thin membrane that you can almost see through, before breaking.

Put the dough back in the bowl and cover it with a damp tea towel. Leave to stand for a couple of hours until doubled in size.

Knock back the dough until it deflates, then give it another quick knead. To make rolls, cut the dough into even pieces. For 'cob' sized rolls, divide the dough by 8, shape into rounds and roll or press a little so they have a diameter of 10cm. Arrange on 2 floured or lined baking trays. For smaller, rounder rolls, divide the dough into 12 or even 16 pieces and shape them into rounds. Again, arrange on 2 baking trays, unless you want them to touch, in which case, space them out over one large baking tray – they will spread towards one another during proving and in the oven. Cover the rolls with a damp tea towel and leave to rise again.

Preheat the oven to its highest setting.

When the dough has risen and the rolls have a well-rounded, springy dome, put them in the oven and bake for 15–20 minutes until they have a well-browned exterior and sound hollow when tapped on the bottom.

Makes 8–16, depending on size

500g strong bread flour, any sort, plus extra for dusting
7g fast-acting yeast
8g salt
1 tbsp sugar or honey or malt extract
about 300ml tepid water

LEMON CURD

This is a good old-fashioned treat and something our mams used to make. There's nothing like it for slathering on to a scone or a teacake or you could use it as a cake filling. Enjoy. Limes and oranges also make lovely curds.

Makes 4 jars

4 eggs
4 egg yolks
200g caster sugar
6 unwaxed lemons, juice of all 6 and zest of 3
150g unsalted butter, cut into small cubes

First prepare the jars. Sterilise them either using a hot dishwasher cycle or wash them in hot, soapy water, rinse thoroughly and dry them out in a low oven. Make sure the jars are completely dry before filling.

Whisk the eggs and egg yolks in a large heatproof bowl until well combined. Add the sugar and stir in the lemon juice and zest. Add the butter, then place the bowl over a saucepan of very gently simmering water, making sure the bottom of the bowl doesn't touch the water.

Stir the mixture with a wooden spoon for 5 minutes until the butter has melted, then cook for 10–12 minutes, whisking constantly. The curd should have the consistency of custard and leave a light trail when the whisk is lifted. It will continue to thicken in the jars.

Pour the hot lemon curd into the sterilised jars and leave to cool. Cover the curd with a disc of waxed paper or baking parchment and seal with a lid. Store in the fridge and use within a couple of weeks.

PROPER CUSTARD

We love some custard with a fruit pie and, as always, home-made is best. The coffee bean, by the way, adds a depth of flavour but doesn't make the custard taste of coffee.

Serves 4–6

250ml whole milk
250ml double cream
1 vanilla pod, split, or
   1 tsp vanilla extract
1 coffee bean (optional)
6 egg yolks
50g caster sugar

Put the milk and cream in a saucepan with the vanilla pod or extract and the coffee bean, if using. Bring the milk and cream almost to the boil, then remove the pan from the heat and set it aside for the flavours to infuse while the mixture cools.

Whisk the egg yolks and sugar together in a bowl until pale and foamy. Reheat the milk and cream, again to just below boiling point. Strain the milk mixture through a sieve into a jug and rinse out the saucepan. Slowly pour the milk mixture over the eggs, whisking constantly as you do so, then pour it all back into the saucepan. Set the pan over a very low heat and stir constantly until the custard has thickened slightly and you can draw a line through it when it coats the back of a spoon.

Strain the custard again and if you aren't serving it immediately, put the vanilla pod, if using, back into it. Cover the custard with cling film, making sure it comes into contact with the surface to prevent a skin from forming. Leave to cool.

MARZIPAN

You can buy marzipan, of course, but it's nice to make your own sometimes to add to a special cake. You can also use it to make little marzipan sweeties. This is a basic recipe and you can add different flavourings, such as a few drops of rose or orange blossom water or a little rum, before adding the egg whites.

Put the ground almonds in a food processor. Process until they start to clump together a little, but still look dry – the texture is a bit like fine couscous. Add the icing sugar to the almonds and continue to process for another couple of minutes, pushing down the sides regularly as the mixture will stick to them.

Add a few drops of almond extract. With the motor running, drizzle in just enough egg white for larger clumps to form. Keep an eye on it and be careful not to over process – if you do, the oil in the almonds will start separating and will make the marzipan look greasy.

When you notice the mixture is clumping, stop processing and squeeze some of the mixture together between your fingers – if it forms a dough, it's done. It will look quite smooth, but the texture will still be a little grainy.

Wrap the marzipan or put it in a container and keep it in the fridge until you need to use it. If it dries out, cover it with a damp tea towel and it will absorb enough moisture to be pliable.

200g ground almonds
85g icing sugar
a few drops of almond extract
2–3 tsp egg white

MINCEMEAT

Obviously you can buy mincemeat for mince pies or our fantastic mincemeat and marzipan twists on page 250, but home-made is a different beast. Takes no time to put together and it's well worth it. It keeps for ages, so if you make it for Christmas, save some for Easter!

Makes about 3 x 450g jars

200g raisins
200g sultanas
100g dried prunes, finely
    chopped
100g dried sour cherries, finely
    chopped (or dried blueberries
    or cranberries)
100g candied peel (preferably
    orange), finely chopped
zest and juice of 2 oranges
100ml sherry (medium sweet,
    such as Amontillado)
75ml brandy or Kirsch
1 Bramley apple, peeled, cored
    and finely diced
1 tsp ground cinnamon
½ tsp ground cardamom
½ tsp ground allspice
a good rasp of nutmeg
1 tbsp orange blossom water
    (optional)
250g light brown soft sugar
100g suet

First prepare the jars. Sterilise them either using a hot dishwasher cycle or wash them in hot, soapy water, rinse thoroughly and dry them out in a low oven. Make sure the jars are completely dry before filling.

Put all the dried fruit – the raisins, sultanas, prunes, cherries and peel – into a large saucepan with the orange zest and juice, then add the sherry and brandy or Kirsch. Bring to the boil, then remove the pan from the heat. Stir thoroughly and leave to stand for an hour.

Add all the remaining ingredients and heat again, this time very gently, until the suet has melted. Spoon into the sterilised jars, then leave to cool before covering. Store somewhere cool and dark and leave for at least 2 weeks but preferably a month before using.

CANDIED LIME ZEST

This is easy to make and is a great topping for the bee sting cake on page 66 or any citrusy bake. It's a really useful part of the home baker's armoury of techniques. The citric acid really helps the acid flavour pop but leave it out if you want a milder taste. You can, of course, use this recipe with any citrus fruit. If you use the citric acid, be sure to look for the food-grade type.

Makes enough to decorate 1 cake

3 limes
100g granulated sugar

To store
75g granulated sugar
¼ tsp food-grade citric acid, ground to a powder (optional)

Pare the zest from the limes in thick strips, then slice the strips thinly.

Put the strips in a small saucepan and cover them with cold water. Bring to the boil, then immediately strain and run the zest strips under cold water. Repeat the boiling and rinsing process, then set the zest aside.

Put the sugar into a saucepan with 150ml of water. Heat slowly, stirring until the sugar has dissolved, then add the zest and bring to the boil. Turn down the heat and simmer gently for 10–15 minutes until the zest is translucent.

Separate the zest from the syrup and spread it out on some kitchen paper. Leave until completely dry – an hour or so will usually be long enough, unless it is very humid, in which case, leave overnight.

To store, mix the sugar with the citric acid, if using, then toss the lime zest in it. Transfer to an airtight container and it will keep indefinitely.

BUTTERCREAM ICING

This is an easy icing to make, but the only problem can be that you end up covered in clouds of icing sugar! The best way round this is to start mixing the sugar and butter really slowly, then speed up once they are more or less combined. The basic formula is always double the amount of icing sugar to butter. Other than that you can vary it as you like.

Make sure the butter is very soft before you start. Put the butter in a bowl with all the icing sugar and very gently stir them together with a wooden spoon. This should stop you getting icing sugar clouds in your kitchen. When the mixture is looking lumpy and is no longer powdery, switch to electric beaters or beat more vigorously. Beat until the mixture is very soft, light and airy.

Add the vanilla extract and beat in a little milk to loosen the mixture – you want a reluctant dropping consistency. Add food colouring if using – just a drop or 2 at a time – right at the end, making sure you beat well in between each addition. Keep adding until you are happy with the colour.

Chill the icing until you need it and beat again to loosen a little before using.

Make enough to ice a regular sandwich cake

200g butter, softened
400g icing sugar
a few drops of vanilla extract
up to 2 tbsp milk
a few drops of food colouring
   (optional)

VARIATIONS

Coffee: Replace the milk with 2 tablespoons of strong coffee.

Chocolate: Add 25g of cocoa powder with the icing sugar. Replace the milk with 100g of dark chocolate, melted and cooled a little.

Citrus zest: Add the zest of 1 lemon or orange or the zest of 2 limes at the start of the recipe.

Jam: Purée 50g of jam, then beat this into the buttercream.

APRICOT JAM

This is one of the nicest of all jams and this method of macerating the fruit with the sugar works really well. You don't have to add any extra water, which means the flavour is more concentrated and you don't have to cook it for long either, as there is less liquid to boil off before reaching the setting point. We've used a bit less sugar than usual, which means that the jam does need to be kept in the fridge once opened.

**Makes about
3 x 340g jars**

750g apricots, pitted and roughly chopped (reserve the stones)
500g jam sugar (with added pectin)
1 lemon (see method)

First prepare the jars. Sterilise them either using a hot dishwasher cycle or wash them in hot, soapy water, rinse thoroughly and dry them out in a low oven. Make sure the jars are completely dry before filling.

Put the apricots in a bowl with the jam sugar. Pare the zest from the lemon, then cut the lemon in half and squeeze out the juice. Add the juice to the apricots and sugar.

Put the lemon zest and any pips from squeezing the lemon on to a square of muslin. Lightly crack the apricot stones so the kernels are exposed and add them to the muslin, then tie the muslin into a parcel and add it to the bowl.

Cover the bowl of fruit with a tea towel and leave it to stand until the sugar has dissolved and the fruit is sitting in liquid.

Before you start cooking the apricots, put a couple of saucers in the freezer to chill. Tip all the fruit, liquid and the muslin bag into a large saucepan or preserving pan, then slowly bring to the boil, stirring regularly. Continue to boil and stir regularly so the fruit cooks evenly, until setting point is reached.

To test for the setting point, use a jam thermometer and for this particular jam it should reach 103°C. If you don't have a thermometer, use the wrinkle test – remove the saucepan from the heat and drop a small spoonful of the jam on to a chilled saucer.

For a soft set, check once the jam has been boiling for about 7 minutes. The aim here is jam with a thick, glossy consistency that doesn't run off the saucer. For a firmer set, check for setting after boiling for 9 minutes – the jam should wrinkle slightly when pushed with a finger. In either case, if the jam is still runny when it hits the saucer, put the pan back over the heat and retest after a couple more minutes.

Remove the muslin bag. Stir the jam to disperse any foam on top, then decant it into the sterilised jars. Put the lids on loosely, then tighten them once the jam has cooled. Store the jam somewhere cool and dark and once opened, store in the fridge and eat within 6 weeks.

CHOCOLATE GANACHE

This is very versatile and can be used as a delicious sauce or as an icing for cakes or can be made into chocolate truffles. Always use equal amounts of chocolate and cream and if you want to include alcohol, add it once the chocolate has melted and made a smooth sauce with the cream.

200ml double or whipping
   cream
200g chocolate (any sort you
   like, or a mixture), chopped
   very finely

Put the cream in a saucepan. Bring it to just below boiling point, then remove the pan from the heat.

Put the chopped chocolate in a bowl. Pour the cream over the chocolate from a height and leave to stand for a few minutes without stirring – the chocolate should melt easily in this time.

Whisk the cream and chocolate together. It should have a pouring consistency at this point and can be used as a sauce. If it starts to thickens as it cools, it can be very gently reheated. Cool to room temperature before chilling.

To turn the chocolate sauce into a thick, spreadable paste that can even be used to make truffles, chill until firm.

To whip the ganache into a thick, voluminous icing for cakes, chill it until firm, then remove it from the fridge. Loosen it up a bit with a spoon, then beat until soft, lighter in colour and very aerated.

BROWN BUTTER

Brown butter, or beurre noisette in French, can be used as a sauce, but it also adds a lovely toasty caramel note to bakes. It's a handy technique to know about and we use it in the cupcakes on page 94.

Prepare the brown butter in advance, as it needs to cool back down to room temperature before being used in a baking recipe. Some of the water evaporates from the butter during the cooking process, so to make 125g of brown butter, you need 160g of unsalted butter. For 200g of brown butter, you need 250g of unsalted butter.

Put the diced butter in a frying pan – if possible, use a light-coloured, enamel-based pan, as it makes it easier to see what's happening.

Heat the butter over a medium heat until it has melted. Bring it to the boil, stirring constantly, until the white milk solids that initially foam at the top of butter, sink and turn brown. They will turn brown very quickly, so don't take your eye off the pan for a moment.

As soon as you see the solids turning brown, remove the pan from the heat and pour the butter into a bowl. Up to you whether you keep the brown bits or not – there is a lot of flavour in them so they are great for baking. Leave to cool until the butter is solid but still very soft – you can speed this up in the fridge if you like. Once cool, it can be used as needed.

INDEX

Mini florentines 244

Great job everyone!

We have to salute the heroism of our team here. While helping us create this book, they have had to munch their way through mountains of pies, cakes, bread and other goodies – it's a tough job but someone has to do it!

A mega shout out then to Catherine Phipps, recipe and all-round cooking guru, Andrew Hayes-Watkins, photographer extraordinaire, Lucie Stericker, talented designer, and Jinny Johnson, wizard with words.

Big thanks to the wonderful Lola Milne and her assistant Hattie Baker, who make all the food look so mouth-watering for the photographs, and to Rachel Vere for all the attractive props. And to Elise See Tai for proofreading and Vicki Robinson for compiling the index.

The team at Orion are always a fantastic support, especially managing director Anna Valentine, our publisher Vicky Eribo, publicists Virgina Woolstencroft and Alainna Hadjigeorgiou, marketers Lynsey Sutherland and Helena Fouracre, sales director, Jennifer Wilson, and Simon Walsh in production.

And many thanks to the lovely people at Ibison Talent Group who always have our backs: our agent Nicola Ibison and Tasha Hall, Roland Carreras and Rosie Money-Coutts.

We love you all.

We'd like to dedicate this book to our mams, who filled our childhoods with the scent of wonderful baking and fantastic memories that we carry with us to this day.

First published in Great Britain in 2022 by Seven Dials,
an imprint of The Orion Publishing Group Ltd
Carmelite House, 50 Victoria Embankment
London EC4Y 0DZ

An Hachette UK Company

1 3 5 7 9 10 8 6 4 2

ISBN (Hardback): 978 1 8418 8433 2

ISBN (eBook): 978 1 8418 8434 9

Publisher: Vicky Eribo
Editor: Jinny Johnson
Recipe consultant: Catherine Phipps
Photography: Andrew Hayes-Watkins
Design & art direction: Lucie Stericker, Studio 7:15
Food stylist: Lola Milne
Food stylist's assistant: Hattie Baker
Prop stylist: Rachel Vere
Proofreader: Elise See Tai
Indexer: Vicki Robinson
Production Manager: Simon Walsh

Origination by F1 Colour Ltd., London

Printed in Germany by
Mohn Media Mohndruck GmbH

More best-sellers from the Hairy Bikers